PRAISE FOR DAVE JACQUES

I'm a recovering Hero. I liked to suggest clever ideas, be seen to be indispensable and receive "thank you's" for my efforts. When people critiqued my ideas, I was defensive. When that failed, I could play the victim. I wish I had Dave's book 30 yrs ago to help my younger self. The Mark of 2024 will put the strategies into action with my coaching clients.

MARK LEVISON - CERTIFIED SCRUM
TRAINER AND AGILE COACH

We've all seen them, relied on them, or acted as them at work: heroes. This book unpacks the hero concept, explains the harm in it (and there's a lot!), and provides advice on creating a healthier environment.

GIL BROZA, AUTHOR OF *DELIVER
BETTER RESULTS AND THE HUMAN SIDE
OF AGILE*

SHATTER THE HERO CULTURE

SHATTER THE HERO CULTURE

ORGANIZATIONAL STRATEGIES TO BOOST TEAMWORK

DAVE JACQUES

TRANSLATED BY
HEIDI RIPPLINGER

SIMPLEMENT COMPLEXE

To all my friends, coaches, mentors, clients, and teachers that have helped me become my best self.

"In a typical organization, most people are doing a second job they are not paid for."

Robert Kegan et Lisa Laskow Lahey, An Everyone Culture: Becoming a Deliberately Developmental Organization

CONTENTS

List of Figures and Tables   xiii
Introduction   xv

1. The Era of Corporate Heroes   1
2. The Dark Side of Heroes   10
3. A Phenomenon That Eats Away at Your
   Company from Within   29
4. Don't Go Hunting for Heroes   40
5. Six Strategies to Outwit Everyday Heroes   45
6. How to End Hero Culture Within the Company   64
7. When I'm the Hero   87
8. Pick the Right Strategies   110
9. Reinventing the Heroic Attitude   121
10. How to Shatter the Hero Culture   138

   Conclusion   147
   Coming Soon   149
   Acknowledgments   151
   Bibliography   153
   Resources   157
   Biography   159

LIST OF FIGURES AND TABLES

Figure 1.1—Three-Phase Approach
Figure 2.1—Karpman's Drama Triangle
Figure 6.1—Planned vs. Real
Figure 6.2—Team Competency Matrix
Figure 9.1—Change Perspective When Faced with Problems
Figure 9.2—From Reactive to Creative Attitudes
Figure 10.1—Three Transformative Phases to Shatter the Hero Culture
Figure 10.2—Phase 1: Shatter the Hero Culture
Figure 10.3—Phase 2: Learn to Work with Heroes
Figure 10.4—Phase 3: Overcome the Need for Heroes

Table 6.1—Heroes' Work Plan
Table 9.1—Persecutor Versus *Challenger*
Table 9.2—Rescuer Versus *Coach*
Table 9.3—Victim Versus *Creator*
Table 9.4—Reactive vs. Creative Behavior
Table 9.5—Adaptability Contains Both Reactivity and Creativity

INTRODUCTION

When people ask me what I do for work, I tend to have the same conversation with each person. The words change a little, but the content stays the same. Here's a perfect example:

What do you do, Dave?

> I'm an organizational coach and facilitator. I help promote teamwork within companies.

Oh yeah? How do you do it?

> I go the extra mile to develop a good team dynamic and improve the company culture. Most importantly, I help coworkers develop the right attitude and behavior. In short, I create true work teams.

Really? I could use this where I work. There are problems with my coworkers and my manager.

> How so?

I'm always overworked. I think my manager doesn't understand that I can't do everything; plus, there is this coworker I can't stand. He complains about everything, and I end up having to do his work for him. I like my job, but I think I should change positions. I feel trapped and I don't think my manager will let me go that easily.

It sounds like you're in a hero culture.

A hero culture?

The hero is the expert, the one who knows everything about how to do the work. The hero is the standout, the reference, the key player everyone needs. No one can work without him. No project can be successful without him. He will undermine any decisions he was not a part of making. He will complain about things going wrong but won't be part of the solution.

You're describing a typical day at my work!

What I call the hero is, in fact, a mindset the members of a company develop while working together. To be the standout and the reference is motivated by the need to be the best. But heroes also have a dark side. They are not perfect, and they develop bad habits that affect their coworkers.

And yet, this is what companies *are seeking.*

People tell themselves, "This is how it works," when working in a company, and they get used to the idea. In fact, companies are dependent on heroes because they couldn't survive without them.

Still, hero culture is a taboo subject. I don't have to explain what it involves for long before the person I'm speaking with finds a similar story. But no one talks about it. There seems to be a consensus on the fact that heroes are present; however, people put up with the situation without discussing it. Talking about heroes shines a light on a problem. It demands major changes in the way companies operate, an effort that's not always easy to make.

This book challenges the taboo and puts forward a new and better way to shatter the hero culture in the workplace. The idea is not to cast heroes aside, but to find a better way of working with them, without the constant pressure to deliver. In time, companies will no longer want to rely on heroes.

CHAPTER 1
THE ERA OF CORPORATE HEROES

> " ... yeah, but Dave, it's like that everywhere.

Each person I talk to about heroes in business

I t never fails. Whenever I describe what a hero is, the effects, and his mindset, someone tells me it's how all companies work. It's how things work from large to small and medium-sized companies (SME). So far, all my clients, regardless of their age, have told me they've experienced this phenomenon in their workplace.

And this phenomenon is not just part of North American culture. I also saw it in Europe and Australia in conferences I hosted, and when giving trainings, or coaching clients. The hero culture is present in companies worldwide.

The more I talk about heroes, the more people find concrete examples in their everyday lives. As I explain the effects that heroes have on the dynamic between coworkers, they tell me, "That's exactly what I'm going through." I am happy to be able to help so many companies, but at the same time shocked to see how widespread the phenomenon is.

HEROES ARE EVERYWHERE

The notion of heroes is well entrenched in our day-to-day lives. Books, for example, are filled with heroic adventures. Movies have franchises based on famous heroes that are blockbusters. Clothing, both for children and adults, displays our favorite heroes. We even go so far as to repeat cliché quotes from heroes in our conversations. As Yoda would say, "Do or do not. There is no try."

Heroes are everywhere in our culture. They inspire us, influence us, and encourage us daily. We want to be like them.

Corporate heroes are as inspirational as they are useful. They are coworkers with great effectiveness and expertise that allow them to address complex situations. Their vast knowledge makes them the first pick in work teams. Without heroes, companies would not be so successful.

But heroes also have a dark side that we see in books and movies: when they decide to fly solo, they fail. Worse than failing, they get severely hurt. They aggravate an already complex situation. They cause major damage, sometimes the death of another character. The hero believes they can do everything alone, without putting their team in danger; however, it's the exact opposite. Next, their best ally tells them something along these lines, "It was really irresponsible to try to fix the situation all alone. Why'd you do that? We're here to help you. We must take this on together." The hero brings their group back together so they can succeed in finding a solution to their problems.

This is a classic scenario, but we never tire of it.

The corporate hero does the same thing: they act on their

own and leave their coworkers in the dark, which causes negative effects in their wake. They collect a string of successes and credits as do the heroes of our bedtime stories.

If this scenario is so familiar, why do we keep repeating it over and over? Because companies are founded on beliefs that promote and support heroes. They encourage employees to adopt a mindset like the hero from the stories.

CHALLENGING THE STATUS QUO

I grew up with the belief that "work is hard," that you must always give it 110%, that it's not a place to enjoy, nor a place for making friends, especially with the management.

These beliefs make up the unwritten rules of a game called "working." These rules force workers to develop means to win, and to be a hero is one of these means. Nevertheless, these unwritten rules are old-fashioned. To win, we must change the rules and strategy.

One of these unwritten rules is that to be productive, you must be busy all the time.

Having a long to-do list and a full schedule is a sign of importance and success. If an employee has free time, you think they could take on a lot more. However, the need to be constantly busy has the opposite effect. When a highway has reached its maximum capacity, you find yourself in a traffic jam: the expected effectiveness never materializes.

The desire to be productive at all costs causes employees to feel guilty when they find a gap in their schedule. This encourages the habit of taking on more work to avoid having to justify what others would perceive as a waste of time. Unsurprisingly, a hero's to-do list is often never-ending. But to be more effective and increase productivity, we must simplify and do less.

Another unwritten rule is that work is hard and complaining about your job is normal.

Employment ads emphasize the exemplary values of the company, the collaborative work culture, and the way the company develops the employees. However, my client conversations center around subjects like burnout, extra hours, being overworked, complicated relationships between coworkers, management's failure to listen, etc. When you compare the employment ad and the reality at work, you could almost claim false advertising. The heroes also reinforce this double-talk. Only companies who question the established hero culture are in the process of solving this problem.

Work does *not* have to stay hard. We should strive to improve it, especially with all the time we invest in it.

High levels of skill and expertise are the most in demand on the market.

To be hired, you must specialize in one single field or niche through hoarding certifications and many years of experience. This way of playing the hiring game ends with pigeon-holing workers in a single field. Therefore, companies lack the ability to adapt when their needs for expertise change.

The expert stays in their niche because if they change, they will no longer be in demand, due to a lack of experience. Experts become the heroes of their niche. They stack certificates on their LinkedIn profile, usually in the form of a lengthy list of acronyms next to their name, which increases the gap between them and the other workers in the same field.

Instead, the expert must be someone who can develop the skills of the employees in the companies, and not the only person who does all the work.

Teamwork is prominent in companies, so it is believed that **everyone can work in a team.**

No, not everyone knows how to work well in a team. This is primarily due to focusing too much on technical expertise. Workers rarely receive training on work relationships and how to communicate with coworkers. In an increasingly digital and remote business, communication skills such as listening, empathy, and collaboration are not prioritized. Still, companies take it for granted that a worker has these skills.

Heroes are no exception: they do not work well in teams. In fact, heroes are not interested in working in teams because their success relies on individual effectiveness. They work better alone. But teamwork is essential for a company to succeed. Simply seating the employees together is no longer enough. Teamwork is key to collective success.

Corporate heroes come from a culture that values the individual, their salary, bonus, title, office, and parking spot. The hero culture will stay in place as long as companies value the individual. To create rewarding and long-lasting work environments, the company must re-examine the unwritten rules.

By no longer relying on heroes, the company becomes more flexible and develops an ability to overcome the difficulties and growing changes of the market.

AN APPROACH TO SHATTER THE HERO CULTURE

Companies must learn how to stop depending on heroes. As soon as a high-level skill is missing, they hire a hero who can deal with the problem single-handedly. The hero will be rewarded for their efforts, and thus start climbing the social ladder, and eventually be replaced by a new generation of heroes. This way of doing business is so deeply embedded in company culture that any approach that leaves out heroes is considered risky.

Changing the company culture is a deliberate act that demands discipline from all employees. Change does not occur with a transition committee who only communicates the results to the employees. A systematic approach is needed to give the company time to change itself.

I developed the following approach over the last few years. It is divided into three phases as you can see in Figure 1.1. The book you're reading focuses on the first phase, which serves as a foundation for the following two phases. Chapter 10 gives more details on the whole approach, integrating the teachings of the book.

Figure 1.1—Three-Phase Approach

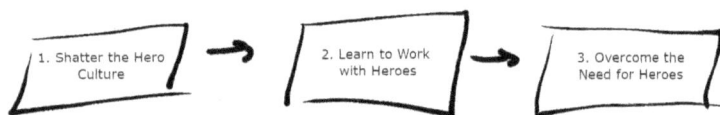

This work is based on Prime/OS™, published as an Open Source, Free Cultural Work via the CC-BY-SA license from Creative Commons. Download the Prime/OS™ Definition Here: http://openspaceagility.com/prime/download-prime/

1. SHATTER THE HERO CULTURE

The objective of this step is threefold: to understand what a hero is, to unveil the hero culture, and to invite the employees to use concrete methods to shatter this culture in their day-today lives. This step ends with a presentation to the company to demystify the hero phenomenon.

Chapters 2 and 3 explain the hero phenomenon's different effects on the employees and the company process.

Methods to shatter the hero culture or at least minimize its effects are explained in Chapters 5, 6, and 7. For major, long-lasting change to occur in a company, concrete actions must be planned and put into place by all employees. All members of the company *must* take part in the transformation process. The approach based on Prime/OS™ leads participants in a series of two Open Space meetings connected to hero culture and includes a learning period between each session.

An Open Space meeting is an opportunity for people to exchange and share about an important topic or issue. All employees are encouraged to be part of the change. This improvement tool helps bring a long-lasting change in the company culture. What makes Open Space meetings successful is that it is based on voluntary participation since a change in culture is unlikely without it.

My approach derives from "Cultural anthropology" (May 7, 2023), namely the study of human beings and human societies, and Dave Gray's book, *Liminal Thinking: Create the Change You Want by Changing the Way You Think* (2016), which allows people to create change in understanding their beliefs and transforming them. A change in the business culture is like a change in society. Therefore, the approach uses these foundations so that its new culture is adapted to the company's reality.

When the hero culture is well understood, and the two Open Space meetings have been held, Phase 1 is complete.

This book does not prepare you for the Open Space meetings necessary to complete Phase 1. However, it allows you to understand the corporate hero culture by using a common language to discuss it in your workplace, while bringing you one step closer to a change in culture. This book is, in fact, a good complement to professional coaching or mentoring.

2. LEARNING TO WORK WITH HEROES

Phase 2 is a time for learning, exploration, and experimentation to discover new ways to work with corporate heroes. The methods practiced in Phase 1 become more natural during Phase 2, where we learn new methods to help us stop, change, and create new company culture. The learning process is the same as Phase 1, with two Open Space meetings, but a longer learning period is accounted for since changing the employees' work process and mindsets is more demanding and time-consuming.

Phase 2 is complete when the series of two Open Space meetings has been successfully completed.

3. GOING BEYOND THE NEED FOR HEROES

Phase 3 is one of mastery. The company no longer needs to regularly hold Open Space meetings. It is mature enough to assess the need for an Open Space meeting on its culture, and it can proceed based on what was learned in previous phases.

The hero culture is successfully shattered, and the company can adapt through healthy mindsets and creative behaviors among its employees. In addition, the company is aware that maintaining a healthy corporate culture requires continuous maintenance and adjustments.

SUMMARY

Heroes are everywhere in our stories, films, and books, including our workplaces. While they bring their own set of advantages, they also have several disadvantages that can undermine teamwork, since a hero is foremost a lone wolf. Work is governed by unwritten rules that support the heroic mindset and prevent us from changing the company culture. For example:

- You must be busy all the time to be productive.
- Work is hard and complaining about work is normal.
- High-level skills and expertise are the most in demand.
- Everyone can work in a team.

These unwritten rules are old-fashioned and must change to shatter the hero culture in companies.

The approach to changing this culture is based on cultural anthropology, namely the study of human beings and human societies. A change in company culture is similar to a change in society. Based on the Open Space technology, the approach contains three phases:

1. Shatter the hero culture: unveil the hero culture, understanding the effects they have in the workplace, and putting into practice concrete methods to curb the harmful effects of heroes in everyday life.
2. Learn to work with heroes: stopping, changing, and creating new ways of doing business to work better with heroes.
3. Overcome the need for heroes: the company maintains their culture regularly with what they learned in Phases 1 and 2.

The next chapter delves into the dark side of heroes, and the harmful effects they have on their colleagues.

CHAPTER 2
THE DARK SIDE OF HEROES

" I wish I could just clone you.

My manager at the time

A t first glance, this statement seems to be a nice way to highlight an employee's efforts and to recognize their significant contribution within the team. However, it also hides a noteworthy aspect: the company could not do without this person. It's as much an expression of fear of losing the employee as an appreciation of their good work. Another version of the same sentence would be, "I don't know what I'd do without you." I was told that so many times I came to believe it.

I remember one time that illustrates this scenario particularly well. I was based in Quebec, and the client had a division in Toronto. I had to be there from time to time to get better acquainted with them and facilitate interactions. It was back when e-meetings weren't very popular.

So, I got up around 3:30 a.m. to call a taxi to take me to the airport. Boarding was set at 5:25 a.m., the first flight of the morning. I had time to work for about an hour on the plane before leaving the airport to take a taxi to the client's offices. I arrived around 9 a.m. For the rest of the day, I was able to understand my customer's issues and needs, explain a concept, establish a solution, quote the work, and explain the terms of the agreement. Even before leaving in the evenings, I was already in the process of completing the work. With luck, I would be back home by 10 p.m. The next day, I had to be at the office at 7 a.m.

Doing it once is not so bad but having to do it every other week is exhausting. The travel time, and especially the feat of accomplishing the work of many people at once, is unsustainable even with accommodations (e.g., leaving Sunday nights and returning Mondays). I told myself that I could manage everything, and I was very efficient. I was the only employee who could do it. But I was dying of a thousand cuts. My social and love life were turned upside down, and I didn't have time for any hobby either.

The problem isn't my ability to do all of this, but the fact that the company relied only on me to do it all, because to ask someone else would cost way too much. And the worst part is that I had accepted this readily by saying, "I'll do it!" My employer and I were both responsible for this situation.

WHAT EXACTLY ISN'T WORKING?

When overextending yourself becomes the norm, you've got to do it all the time: always faster, always more efficiently. Companies have adapted themselves to support the hero by adjusting some processes in place that favor heroic mindsets like recruitment, pay scales, career plans, or managerial style. They want these one-of-a-kind employees more and more: it's addictive. Being a hero then becomes more and more sought after and encouraged.

Ever since my first job, being efficient, getting the job done quickly, achieving more with less, always outperforming targets, and constantly growing have always been important and a priority. This obsession with productivity created an environment where the only way to survive was to become a hero and develop superpowers to overcome all the challenges.

Nevertheless, not everyone can become a full-time hero, or even on occasion. It's like putting the pedal to the metal permanently and hoping to go even faster. Since some people succeed at it, it's expected that others can do the same by repeating the same ways of doing things that have been named, "best practices." More than once, I've been asked to explain my "recipe for success." It's simple:

1. Work alone.
2. Keep the information to yourself.
3. Don't take vacations.
4. Work outside business hours.
5. Make it so they can't do it without you.
6. Be the only person who can solve a problem.
7. Endure your hardships.
8. Think that no one can do what you do.
9. Obtain the most individual credit possible.
10. Do not ask for help.

Not the recipe you were thinking of? It's probably also not as tempting as all the others who have already been published at any rate. To be efficient, I relied on individual autonomy, and it worked! The problem wasn't being a hero but being one full-time. It had become my default way of doing things.

Over time, I've observed that being a hero created collateral damage around me. There's not only success to consider; the consequences affected my well-being, the people around me, and my work environment. My personal life suffered because my mindset toward work wielded an influence over my entire life. And like many people, I spent an incalculable amount of time at work. I refused to believe that a clear-cut boundary was possible between my professional life and my personal life.

It took me many years to understand the dark side of being a hero. At first, I believed I was simply gifted and better than the others. In fact, this satisfied my need for approval and gratification: it was like getting a report card from school. In the workplace, it's promotions and pats on the back that are our report card. That was what I believed at the time.

I saw coworkers avoid me, to not have to put up with me every day. They did not want to bow to my will, suffer from my mood swings, but mostly, stay in the shadow of my hero cape. It's an overwhelming observation when you think about it. I must say I still feel a great deal of shame with respect to my heroic mindset. However, far from being only my mea culpa, this phenomenon must be seen in its entirety to be well understood.

WHAT DOES THE DARK SIDE OF A HERO LOOK LIKE?

Karpman's Drama Triangle is going to help us better understand what a hero is. This model, which has been around since the 70s, is rather simple for understanding the different facets of a hero.

Developed by the psychiatrist Stephen B. Karpman (n.d.), Karpman's Drama Triangle is a psychological model for understanding the dynamic of some relationship problems. It helps single out the mindsets that people can adopt in their everyday lives, whether at work or at home. It also allows us to define the different types of heroes that exist. Without being exhaustive, the model labels character traits and behaviors to observe them better later. It uses three positions that people adopt to protect themselves, to take advantage of a situation, to defend themselves, or to go on the offensive. The more emotionally charged the situations are, the more noticeable and stronger the positions are. The three positions are dynamic: people change them according to the situation or for their benefit. Our heroes are experts in the execution of this model without even being familiar with it.

THE PERSECUTOR

The Persecutor is the one who imposes himself and his views on those around him. People have more bad things than good to say about this type of hero who takes everything for granted and prevents others from progressing. Others will seek his authorization or risk having him overrule decisions made in his absence. The Persecutor is also the one who will keep work for himself, saying, "This is for me," or, "Only I can do this part."

The hero persecutes his team by taking over all the work and leaving little behind. His ideas are always the best and his favorite expression is, "yes, but" (more on this later). The Persecutor has the power and the influence to make himself heard, exercising his right to veto discussions. His presence is generally required in meetings. He's often the center of conversation, even when he's not present! This type of hero tends to be conservative in his decisions since they're based on his knowledge of the subject and rely on his own experiences to support his claims. Reluctant to accept help, even if the intentions are good, he imposes his own on others, insinuating himself into tasks not assigned to him.

I can think of many examples of meetings postponed because only one person was absent even when everyone else was there on time. There is this little awkward moment where everyone looks at each other and gives up by saying, "Cancel the meeting?" The meeting must be rescheduled several days, maybe weeks later. When the Persecutor is there however, and somebody else is missing at the next meeting, he will say, "We will hold the meeting anyway."

The Persecutor is a disruptive element: he short-circuits the process and imposes his law. People adapt to him at the expense of others.

THE RESCUER

The Rescuer is the most common and most appreciated in companies. He's extremely popular because people really like his I-can-do-anything attitude. He can be sent to correct a situation that requires the attention and skills of several people. He's known for his flexibility and efficiency. He also has the talent to straighten out situations. So, he's very effective in crises. All these factors make the team dependent on him. Without him, it would be impossible to handle complex situations. He's often a recognized expert in his field where that expertise becomes a bargaining chip. This hero can use the chip to obtain favors such as a promotion, a new title, or to be assigned to a coveted project. The Rescuer loves telling success stories in which he is the main character. In addition, the Rescuer is ready to hang on to the situation even when he's not needed.

Rescuers are very inspiring. They are associated with positive events and achievements. We often consider them as mentors or examples to follow. They are so inspiring that we end up comparing ourselves (or being compared) to them, and then we wonder how we could become like them to receive the same praise. Like all the heroes, the Rescuer likes the awards and congratulations, whether it's being named employee of the month, getting a bigger annual bonus, a promotion, being featured in an internal article, or any other means of gaining visibility and exercising a greater influence around them.

Rescuers can be found everywhere. I can easily spot them in work teams, especially those responsible for a launch. This stage involves making the latest updates available to customers, such as a new version of a website or an app. Because of the sophistication of the tools and processes involved, the members of this team often must do a lot of sleight of hand and invest a great deal of time outside normal working hours to achieve a successful launch.

One time, I saw an email from a director that said, "Congratulations! The launch took 19 hours. It wasn't easy, but we did it!" That's an extremely long time. The people did this work over the weekend without a break. The next month, another similar email was sent—it had become the norm. Today's best practices allow for this type of production to be done much more quickly. However, companies don't invest in improving the way they do things because there are Rescuers who succeed by putting in the extra effort needed.

Betting on Rescuers means living paycheck to paycheck: you don't know if you have the means to make it through the month, but you manage to make ends meet after all. The challenges are always present, and the company knows for a fact that a hero will show up at the right moment or time to fix the situation.

THE VICTIM

> You're good at what you do Dave. Don't change.

Saying no is difficult for the Victim. His work is so essential that his coworkers hope he stays in the same job indefinitely, making him a victim of his success. This hero tells the same stories as the Rescuer by saying how difficult the situations were and how much he suffered in the process. The Victim complains to get sympathy from others. He critiques the way things work and demands that others change to improve his situation. Others are often the problem and there is only one victim in "The Company." People's attention is on the Victim as much as possible. Despite himself, the hero ends up trapped in a gilded cage.

There is power in victimization. It's simple: you're not responsible for anything. You can complain and attract attention for as long as it remains this way. Accountability becomes a pet peeve.

The Victim wouldn't change the situation even if he was given the chance because his power of influence and sympathy would end. He demands a lot of attention, more than the average person, and he does so at the expense of others.

A typical example of a Victim is when there is somebody who's good at what they do and irreplaceable. Without him, there would be a void difficult ¾ impossible ¾ to fill. For example, when I wanted to change positions and learn a new skill, my manager would say, "You're fine where you are Dave. I need you here." This comforting sentence is also very telling: any attempt at change would be perceived as a threat to the company's fragile stability. I was trapped at my desk, doomed to never grow beyond the limits allowed, resulting in more complaining from me. The Victim winds up as the person who makes us sigh and say, "Him again…"

THE PERSECUTOR—RESCUER—VICTIM DYNAMIC

Figure 2.1—Karpman's Drama Triangle

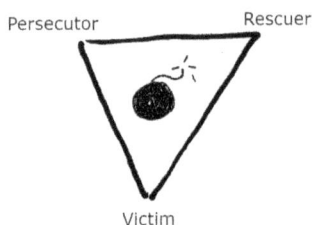

When I discovered this model, I realized I was already familiar with these three positions. I adopted them at specific times and in predictable ways. For example, when I was in a decision-making meeting, I'd have a solution at hand, typical of a Rescuer position. As soon as the opportunity presented itself, I'd save the day with a ready-made solution, bragging about its merits. Whenever someone exposed its flaws or proposed alternative ideas, I'd go into persecutor mode to refute them. I would assert my position by saying "yes, but," "I've done it before and it worked," "I'm the only one who's done this before," "At the end of the day, I'm the one responsible." In short, I would do anything to get my way.

When things didn't work out, or my manager decided otherwise, I instantly went into Victim mode. I would gladly point out all the flaws in their decisions. I would make sure to warn every one of the risks by saying: "I knew it…." With these positions firmly anchored in me, I was able to switch from one to another as easily as a well-trained actor. Even if I adopted the right position for a given situation, I realized I had a default position, which is also a characteristic of our corporate heroes. This position is a center of gravity, drawing the hero back to his normal state. In my case, it was the Rescuer position: it was my best way of dealing with the problem. Once I stopped complaining about the heavy workload I had on my plate, I told myself that the only way out was to solve everything myself. It was the most natural position for me, best received by others because then there would be tangible results. My managers had rather have me solve problems than complain.

The three positions in Karpman's Drama Triangle are symbiotic because they are dependent on each other. To be effective, a Rescuer needs both a Persecutor and a Victim. The same principle applies from one position to another.

Here's an example where the three positions complement each other.

A coworker criticizes my work for not following the rules and asks me to start over. Stunned, I argue by saying I've done what I was asked to do with the information provided. My coworker calls me back, and I keep arguing. My coworker and I are deadlocked, and I call in our manager to decide whether I should really start over.

- **Persecutor**: the Persecutor is my coworker who criticizes me.
- **Victim**: I'm the Victim defending myself.
- **Rescuer**: to break the deadlock, I include our manager as the Rescuer.

The three positions can be people, situations, or concepts (real or imaginary). An example I often hear is "The company doesn't want to," as if we were giving a social entity human form and attributing choices and values to it. We complain we can't make changes without approval or clear direction. When the hero adopts one position, it causes a chain reaction setting off the two other positions whether voluntarily or instinctively. The dynamic doesn't work without all three positions working simultaneously.

"Of course, if a person playing Victim does not find anyone around to rescue or persecute him or her, they will change their environment to find someone else to "play" with." (Karpman, S. 2014)

SOME EFFECTS OF HEROES IN THE COMPANY

As in all businesses, there are problems of every kind. Even if these are not all tied to heroes, the latter are never far away. Here are six situations where you can observe heroic behavior.

1. HAVING LITTLE AVAILABILITY

"I don't have time!"

"I don't know when I'll be able to do this…"

The hero, more likely the Rescuer, has a fully booked schedule and is rarely available when needed. When the time comes to book a meeting or to ask for his help, you are competing with his tight schedule.

The hero gets bombarded with multiple requests from many people daily, which quickly becomes out of control. It's not unusual for the hero to have three or four simultaneous meetings on his schedule. He can't figure out which request to refuse because everything seems important. People also invite him without checking his availability. He rarely has any, but "let's take a chance!" Working online has only magnified this problem, as people are only a click away from the next meeting. There's no more downtime between meetings for changing rooms, floors, or buildings. The schedule is optimized down to the minute. There are apps to manage the schedule and virtual tools to lend a hand, but these tools only put a Band-Aid on a broken arm.

It's very frustrating for the hero. Not only does he have to respond to all these requests on his own, but also, he will be unable to do it in the desired timeframe. Requests are postponed and meetings cut short so he can get to the next faster. Lunchtime is shortened, or work shifts start early and end later. In the end, everyone must make do with a fragment of the hero's value. "We'll take what's left."

2. FIGHTING OVER HEROES

A busy hero means fighting to get them on your team. If he can't prioritize time on his own, people will fight over him for his time. This is what job security looks like for him. It undermines the company, but it's useful for the hero; therefore, he wants to keep the status quo. Heroes are the most sought-after "resources" in the company. It's no wonder that their names are generally well known. They are crucial for managing project risk and guarantee its success because they are reliable, fast, and efficient. Some people see them as the only way to succeed. This results in multiple negotiations before the start of projects to secure the necessary heroes; schedules are often delayed or compromised.

When negotiating fails, we borrow the hero, cannibalizing another project or team. This weakens work teams, distrusts their dynamic, and compromises productivity in favor of another project. Generally, borrowing a hero will come with the following excuses: "We'll make an exception this time,"

"We'll tighten our belts and do our part," "We have no choice," "I have an understanding with management," or "It's out of my hands."

Here's what would happen if we used all three positions of Karpman's Drama Triangle. The Rescuer would prefer to lead the highest-profile activity. Due to his past achievements, he doesn't rely on self-promotion—others do it for him. With this said, he can influence the planning team to get the tasks he wants to work on. And then there is a "despite himself" Rescuer who gets assigned to do the job because the company trusts he can save the day. He has no say whatsoever in this decision.

The Persecutor would probably have orchestrated the change himself. He understands who is needed to make it all happen: either himself or another Rescuer. He has a direct influence on who gets assigned to a project, since he's part of the hush-hush conversations on the subject.

The Victim learns where he is assigned once a decision has been reached. This hero would not be part of the discussion and would grumble that he should have been. He endures the change, whether it's losing the Rescuer who helped him or having to leave for another work assignment.

I've experienced all these positions.

3. NOT ASKING FOR LEAVE

Having a hero around is reassuring, and not having one hurts. Both the team and the manager are nervous about getting by without him, no matter how short his leave may be. For a hero, asking for leave is a challenge. He is irreplaceable. No guidelines or standard operating procedures (if they exist!) would be enough to help the person in charge of taking over his role. Generally, limiting the duration of his leave to avoid further damage is what companies do. If he needs to take several weeks off, he will still work remotely and be available to ensure a smooth process.

I witness this phenomenon every summer, but also at the beginning of the year, or when a hero has planned a vacation outside these two times. The hero's presence is so important that the company can't get along without him for long. At least, that's what they think.

4. BEING OVERSPECIALIZED

Today's job market is highly focused on skill development, whether at the academic, continuing education, or corporate certification level. Career advancement demands us to further develop a defining set of skills. Our resume becomes a business card listing our skills to explain what we do.

The corporate hero will naturally upskill in his role, where his skills will be recognized throughout the company and beyond. His expertise sets him apart and safeguards his role. Few people can oppose or contradict him because of the influence he derives from it.

The challenge with over-specialized heroes is to keep them consistently busy. When a team needs a new specialist, HR will look for another hero. Due to the rapidly changing needs of technologies and business, this becomes a never-ending cycle. This also promotes scarcity which in turn makes it harder to fill highly skilled positions. Corporate heroes are aware they are not one of a kind because others in the market share similar knowledge. They find a position and let the bidding war work for them, which turns out to be a lucrative game.

Many people talk about standing out in the crowd, but what happens is that high-level skills hold a company hostage. Companies can't always fill all the specialized roles they need and must make do with what is available. As a result, a company is unable to launch high-priority projects for lack of specialists.

5. TAKING UP ALL THE SPACE

The corporate hero likes to occupy all the space: physically, emotionally, and verbally. He needs it to play his role to the fullest. It's a constant struggle for him to keep his standing.

Taking up all the space leaves only background roles for others; the hero's immediate circle ends up in the shadows. When the time comes to think of someone to solve a problem, the hero's name comes up first, even if there are other qualified people who could do it. It's very difficult for the others around the hero to develop and expect the same level of success.

Here's how the positions of Karpman's Drama Triangle work in this context. The Persecutor uses his "God-given rights." He claims to be the only one who can do it, or that he's already begun, so passing the job on to someone else is inefficient and simply out of the question.

The Rescuer overprotects people by micromanaging them. He is the first to say, "I'll take care of it!" If someone has been able to say it before him (good luck with that!), the Rescuer will insinuate himself by saying, "I'll pitch in too."

The Victim needs convincing and tremendous reassurance. Each of their concerns must be considered (and there are many!).

Occupying all the space is one of the most common symptoms in every company role. I have witnessed many good team members become managers and not be able to let go of their previous role. They continue performing old duties and making decisions despite the competent team already in place.

6. COMPARING YOURSELF WITH OTHERS

We can't help it: we inevitably compare ourselves to others. Comparing yourself to a hero is usually discouraging. They seem to be in a league of their own. Yet the hero is in the same ballpark as the rest of us.

This phenomenon can often be seen in team sports. A talented player seems to play solo and doesn't give two cents about his teammates. For a while, this player will have success, until he's confronted with opponents that possess great teamwork. He will lose, and so will his team. The same is true of the company hero.

The people around the hero are barely able to shine in both annual evaluations and individual performance reviews. These people are skilled but are compared to the hero who possesses a higher level of expertise and performance.

Implementing productivity measurement tools meets resistance. I constantly find myself taking the time to explain the advantages and especially the proper ways to use these data without fueling fear of misuse. Most people have experienced unpleasant, even life-changing, situations when compared to others. I've even seen them sabotage data to make it seem obsolete. No one wants to be vulnerable, knowing that there will be consequences. Therefore, I must be tactful and rebuild their trust in productivity measurement tools that will make them work for them.

WHAT DOES IT TAKE TO BE A HERO?

Being a hero is foremost a mindset springing from the following behaviors:

1. Working alone.
2. Keeping information to yourself.

3. Not taking vacations.
4. Working outside business hours.
5. Making yourself indispensable.
6. Being the only person who can solve a problem.
7. Enduring your hardships.
8. Thinking that no one can understand what you do.
9. Getting as much individual credit as possible.
10. Not asking for help.

For example, a coworker constantly working alone doesn't mean they are automatically a corporate hero. But working solo on tasks, skipping meetings, or avoiding team interactions, will limit work team collaboration.

A coworker is more likely to develop a heroic position, whether Persecutor, Rescuer, or Victim, the more they exhibit the above behaviors. Keep in mind that the three heroic positions are interdependent. Even if a coworker doesn't showcase all the hero positions at first, a dynamic will set in and develop rapidly over time.

SUMMARY

Heroes can be found in every company. They are part and parcel of our daily lives, and we depend on them. We need to discuss this phenomenon by putting it into words. Using Karpman's Drama Triangle is one way of recognizing heroic positions and raising awareness.

The three heroic positions to understand the hero:

- **Persecutor**: He imposes his rules, and we must adapt to him.
- **Rescuer**: We need him more and more because he's always there to save the day.

- **Victim**: He focuses his attention only on what's going wrong, and he's not responsible for anything.

Noticeable consequences of the hero:

- The hero's availability is tricky to manage daily, and it creates delays.
- The staff will snatch up the heroes' time, cannibalizing it among their own projects.
- Overspecialization creates a scarcity that holds companies hostage.
- The hero takes up all the space at the expense of the people around him.
- Nothing can be gained by comparing oneself to the hero. His teammates always seem inferior, even if they are competent in their respective fields.

Conditions for becoming a hero:

Several behaviors are conducive for developing a heroic position, such as always working alone, enduring hardship, never asking for help, or making oneself indispensable. The key is whether these behaviors can be systematically seen feeding one or more heroic positions within the same coworker.

PRACTICE

How to practice and recognize positions in the workplace:

- Who was the Persecutor, Rescuer, and Victim at your last meeting?
- Have you heard any catchphrases or sentences that sound like the Persecutor, Rescuer, or Victim?

- Do you tend to use any heroic positions?

At this point, you're beginning to understand the kind of behaviors that heroes adopt, and more importantly, how they relate to familiar workplace issues. However, this is only the tip of the iceberg. In the next chapter, we'll see that the perverse and harmful effects on the business extend beyond the hero.

CHAPTER 3

A PHENOMENON THAT EATS AWAY AT YOUR COMPANY FROM WITHIN

t was late on a Friday. Practically everybody had left except one coworker and me. I was trying to get a few more things done before leaving for the weekend. I *finally* had peace and quiet, and I could concentrate. I was frustrated, exhausted, and fed up with having to run into dozens of problems and falling behind during the week. I was juggling two separate roles simultaneously.

My coworker asked me quite a simple question about what she should do with another coworker's timesheet. My reaction was immediate: "What do you mean, it's not clear? You just have to put it in…"

All my frustration and my fatigue came through in my response. I was wondering why she was still asking me that question. I had no desire to help her or interrupt my work, especially not at that hour! I remember her answering with her little shaky voice, awkwardly trying to apologize and justify herself. Her interrupted breathing was tainted with an emotion that my heart understood before my brain did.

She was crying.

My coworker didn't deserve to bear the brunt of my pent-up frustration and burnout. I'd gone too far in my quest for efficiency, and the Persecutor had taken over.

In the previous chapter, we saw hero positions that are easily identifiable in a wide range of situations. This chapter exposes seemingly noble business practices, but which have been perverted by hero addiction. There are others, but the following are all you need for a more complete picture of the phenomenon.

1. TALENT ACQUISITION

"Ready for a new adventure?" This is almost exclusively how the job offers I receive start, followed by a long list of benefits —anything to lure me into a supposedly greener garden.

The search for "talent" is a trend I see a lot, especially on LinkedIn. Recruiters even use titles like "Talent Acquisition Specialist" or other derivatives. They like resumes, relevant experience, knowledge, and certifications. People aren't looking for a person, only talents.

Specialists recruit targeted talents, not individuals. A candidate with targeted talents may have a mindset that doesn't coincide with corporate culture. Higher value is placed on the talent in question rather than the candidate's values and attitudes. Companies experience difficulties in finding candidates who share the same values and attitudes. Frédéric Laloux (2014) discusses this topic in his book *Rein-venting Organizations: A Guide to Creating Organizations Inspired by the Next Stage of Human Consciousness*.

Another word is "acquisition." What does hiring someone have to do with acquisitions? It's not as if you select your product off the shelf. Still, it's what is highlighted on every resume. Hiring someone is about creating a two-way collabo-rative partnership. It has nothing to do with an employer "owning" the talents of its employees.

Actually, talent acquisition specialists are people looking for corporate heroes. To land a job, you must write a heroic resume. You tell yourself, "That's how it works."

2. HEROIC CAREER

The corporate hero likes to change jobs frequently. He has a growth target like the company. Once he's perfected his job or reached his limitations, he searches for a better one. The reasons behind the hero's change are not healthy; he's in search of influence, visibility, financial gain, and power. This is the opposite of the noble phrases that recruitment ads tell us: "Come make a difference with us." What the hero really wants to know is "How much will I earn and what powers will I have?" Enticing money and power elements make the job description secondary.

We measure success by high salary and decision-making powers. We use these two criteria to explain our success to family and friends. Haven't you heard the cliché of the mother who wants her child to be a doctor or lawyer to guarantee their success? The mother hopes for her child to have a good salary and influence, for both her and her child.

In my career, I've never had anyone ask me the straightforward questions, "How much will I make?" and "How much power will I have in the company?" While these are two key points to discuss, that's not how an interview works. If it did, you'd think the hero didn't care about his involvement in the company.

In fact, when the hero applies for a job, he strongly believes he deserves it. However, he plays the interview game explaining that he's a good "team player," supporting the company's values, and highlighting how his skills are relevant to the company's success. In my opinion, this is all smoke and mirrors.

3. HEROES BEGET HEROES

> I'll show you how it really works.

FROM ONE HERO TO A FUTURE HERO

Before changing positions, a corporate hero trains the next generation of heroes, to ensure a suitable successor will continue his work, someone worthy of inheriting his knowledge under his wing. It's usually a coworker from his inner circle, who demonstrates a similar mindset. The hero chooses his own replacement and makes recommendations to management to avoid having someone else imposed on him.

A common corporate practice is to use a mentoring system in which a junior coworker is paired with a senior associate. The practice itself is excellent; however, the hero uses it to train others in his own likeness. This is a sneaky way of doing things under the radar since it's part of a well-known practice authorized by the company. The hero can freely pass on his way of thinking to his replacement.

I recall one meeting where I witnessed this situation in action. I was with a coworker and our task was to present new market best practices to two coworkers: the hero and his mentee. As the conversation progressed, the hero became increasingly reluctant to the new practices. He turned to his mentee and said: "You see how important it is not to be influenced by this way of thinking. Our practices are already just fine."

In a blink of an eye, he had just rejected the widely used best practice in the industry. Despite our willingness to help, he simply wanted to safeguard his knowledge and expertise *without* embracing change. The hardest part to witness was how the hero passed on his reluctance for change to his mentee. My coworker and I exchanged a look of disbelief. At that moment, we simultaneously realized that a new hero was born!

4. THE ILLUSION OF MULTITASKING

I spent years trying to manage multiple requests at the same time. It was a nightmare, I consistently dealt with 5, 10, or even 20 requests at once. I wasted an enormous amount of time searching for an efficient way of coping. In the end, I just couldn't do it.

Job ads frequently ask for candidates who can "multi-task." However, efficient multitasking is an illusion. The hero *pretends* he can do it. When tasked with several jobs at once, he loses valuable time by switching back and forth to "get back into the groove." This wasted time is not initially considered. Instead, it's assumed that each task can be efficiently performed one after another. However, unforeseen events and delays can interrupt the workflow and become distractions such as missing information, a ringing telephone, etc.

When a company attempts to optimize the workload of all its employees, the same problem affects the entire team. Henrik Kniberg's video, "The Resource Utilization Trap" (Crispagileacademy, n.d.) (See Resource section), explains the effects of multitasking and associated costs.

Kniberg (2011) suggests an exercise, the Multitasking Name Game (see Resource section), which illustrates the impact of time lost between tasks. The exercise involves writing a list of first names using two different methods: 1) write all the names at once (multitasking mode), and 2) write one name at a time. The last time I ran this exercise at a client's office, there was a 700% increase in extra time required using the multitasking mode, despite the help of heroes to speed things up.

With the three dynamic positions of Karpman's Drama Triangle, this is what happens with multitasking. For the Persecutor, multitasking is a necessity. He doesn't see any issues because he just needs to manage his time more efficiently, and the "estimated" figures will be respected. "You find that everywhere, so just go with it."

The Rescuer uses his power to complete many tasks simultaneously. He's aware of the problems with multitasking, but he copes with it too.

The Victim complains and tells his coworkers that it's inefficient.

At one point, I decided to bring the problem to light to my manager. I pulled out a complete list of 45 current requests with their waiting times. I outlined all the reasons why the team couldn't be efficient in a lengthy email. I wanted to corner him and prove I was correct, to which he replied, "If you have time to write that kind of email, you're not really busy!" I never bothered to complain about it to that manager again, even though it had a negative impact on my daily work life.

5. FAILURE AND ERRORS DON'T EXIST

Heroes and failures don't mix. A hero avoids any failing scenario at all costs because mistakes threaten his title. For each hero position, the attitude toward failure is different. The Rescuer thrives on impossible scenarios, so failure is not an option. The Persecutor never risks getting into such trouble (others are the problem). The Victim is like a prophet who foresees all the future problems.

The hero has no time for failure and mistakes. He's expected to be consistently good, out of the gate. He showboats his success and hides his mistakes. He remains in control without showing his difficulties and doubts. If there are any mistakes, they are corrected without ever mentioning them. The company counts on him: a failing hero is quickly replaced by a promising successor.

As a hero, I spent a lot of time correcting my mistakes behind closed doors. I really felt there was no margin for error. As the expert, I needed to have the right answers for every question to set a good example. Statements like "You're the expert" or "That's why I hired you" reinforced this feeling.

The right to make mistakes is not something I observe in the companies I work with. Not that it's forbidden, on the contrary. However, employees feel that they can't be allowed to make mistakes, because they have had a bad experience before, or they never witness their coworker make them.

Mistakes are part of the learning process. To master something you must try, fail, and try again. With practice you get better. These mistakes are crucial to learn, even for the corporate hero. But the hero avoids making his mistakes well known; he's an expert. He also believes his coworkers will think of him as unreliable. Yet, his coworkers would benefit from seeing his failures and learn from his mistakes. The hero should make mistakes a normal stage of learning, even for experts.

Companies are increasingly promoting the notion of the "learning organization." But at the same time, they're overlooking the best way to achieve it. They want good people right away, skipping the time needed to develop them. This need for instant expertise limits the opportunities for someone with no job experience to enter the market, or for an expert looking to change their field of expertise.

Accepting mistakes as part of the learning process is a mindset that must be learned. Carol S. Dweck (2006) explains in her book, *Mindset: The New Psychology of Success,* that this mindset is developed by adopting a growth mindset, rather than a fixed mindset. A growth mindset is based on the following principles:

1. Abilities and talents can grow.
2. Learning is essential.
3. Experimentation is valued.
4. Challenges are welcomed.
5. Mistakes equal lessons.
6. Resilience is key to coping with difficulties.

The hero is mostly in a fixed mindset, where mistakes are seen as blemishes on his journey.

Life is not just a series of successes. Mistakes, setbacks, and failures are all part of the journey. Robby Slaughter (2010) explores this nicely in his book, *Failure: The Secret to Success*. Slaughter says that "true failure is when you stop trying."

Mistakes and setbacks are inevitable. If we focus on not making mistakes, we place our attention on avoidance rather than learning from them. You have to fail multiple times before you can hope to succeed; this persistence allows you to learn and grow.

6. DISCOURAGE CHANGE AND INNOVATION

" It's always worked this way.

This is a typical phrase used by heroes. I read it in books warning us about the danger it represents. Accepting change and innovation is a threat to the hero. It means adding more activities, learning new things, and wasting valuable time. The hero prefers not to change the status quo, he wants to wait to see if change is necessary rather than be proactive about it. Being proactive is expensive and doesn't come with instant gratification on his success.

The hero discourages attempts at improvement that he considers nonessential or aren't his own. The more the hero criticizes his coworkers' ideas, the less and less they come up with new ideas. New employees, fresh out of school and full of new ideas, find their excitement for the job snuffed out within weeks. These new employees either accept this reality or leave the company shortly thereafter.

Creativity and innovation require a fostering environment where it's normal to experiment with new ideas. It takes both investment and support from companies to create this kind of environment. However, most companies invest in optimizing their employees' time, with a fast-approaching set deadline. Employees are encouraged to try out new things on their own time, without pay. The employee is then forced to do innovative work outside normal working hours.

Even though some workplaces allow "thinking time," employees feel guilty about the lack of productivity. They'll set aside a half hour on Friday afternoons, to generate ideas quickly to avoid "wasting" time. This famous "thinking time" is the first to be cut if the smallest thing comes up.

In this type of environment, people can't develop their skills and new ideas are few and far between. The hero maintains an image of productivity that's unrealistic to follow.

7. THE INVINCIBLE HERO

Strongly anchored in my heroic mindset, I realized something: I was invincible. I established a solid reputation as a Rescuer, who could guarantee the success of any project. I could break all the rules set in place.

I could say or do anything without consequences. I was convinced that the company would never even think for a second to fire me. I received an occasional slap on the wrist, but nothing that negatively impacted my salary, power, or influence within the company.

I could ask for favors, impose my will, use offensive language, belittle someone, or place blame on a coworker. The worst thing was I could purposely use these strategies to get whatever I wanted. Fortunately, I realized just how inappropriate this mindset was. The problem was the company supporting my improper behavior. My managers would minimize the negative impact of my actions on my coworkers and apologize for me.

The company is willing to accept this type of mindset as long as the hero succeeds. It absolves him of responsibility, placing more of a value on his results than on how he achieves them. *This* is how the corporate hero achieves invincibility.

SUMMARY

Corporate heroes operate at all levels, whether individually, in a close-knit circle, or in the company at large. Even if we greatly value the results they deliver, this leads to problems that eat away at the company from within, thereby creating an unpleasant and harmful culture.

These invisible but very real effects include:

- Recruitment that focuses on finding a hero at the expense of the preferred company culture
- The salary and power that drive the hero's career
- The hero who trains the next generation of heroes
- Ineffective multitasking that creates the illusion that the hero can do it all

- The cover-up of failure and mistakes that deprives the company and staff of necessary learning
- Change and innovation that are discouraged by heroes
- Invincible heroes who do not accept the consequences of their actions

Before continuing our journey into the hero culture phenomenon, let's take a step back. The next chapter will help us reflect on the three hero positions and the effects described so far.

CHAPTER 4
DON'T GO HUNTING
FOR HEROES

t's easier to identify the heroes in your business once you've discovered the three hero positions and their effects. However, you must resist the temptation to go hunting for them. Corporate heroes have a heroic mindset to survive in their work environment. Humans adapt to their environment, and acting heroically is a result of this ability to adapt.

The following sections allow us to reflect on the content covered in the first chapters and avoid quickly judging the heroes around us.

USE THE THREE POSITIONS TO EXPLAIN, NOT JUDGE

When I first discovered Karpman's Drama Triangle with the positions of Persecutor, Rescuer, and Victim, I immediately began to see them in my coworkers, friends, and family. I identified everyone's position and checked to see if I acted the same way in my own work. I was quick to judge without understanding the situation, so I stopped labeling those around me. I was judging people rather than their actions.

You shouldn't start pointing fingers at people. Simply because you recognize an attribute, or a coworker has said something like "it's out of my control," doesn't mean you can place them in a certain position, as I mentioned in previous chapters.

The goal of the three positions is to explain the hero dynamics. Labels can be hurtful. The best way to use them is simply by saying you are "witnessing heroic behavior." It's important to explain the three positions to coworkers before discussing them. This'll help avoid incorrect observations.

PRACTICE

Take a moment and write down your thoughts on the three hero positions: Persecutor, Rescuer, and Victim. Here are a few questions to guide this process (see the template available in the Resource section):

- What heroic behaviors do I observe in my workplace?
- For each behavior identified, which position is the most appropriate: Persecutor, Rescuer, or Victim?
- Do I behave like a hero? If so, which position do I adopt?
- How are the three positions useful in my workplace? What do they help me to achieve?

RECOGNIZE THE EFFECTS OF HEROES IN YOUR WORKPLACE

The effects described in Chapters 2 and 3 are the most common in the workplace, depending on the type of company you work for. SMEs, public, and government organizations do not have the same internal processes as a large company. Some heroic actions may not be as strong as others. If certain heroic effects are not present within your company, you may be able to avoid them with this knowledge.

PRACTICE

Here are a few questions to help you recognize the effects in your company (see template available in the Resource section):

1. What effects have you observed in your company? Circle them.

- Complicated availability
- Hero extraction
- Avoiding absences
- Overspecialization
- Taking up all the space
- Comparing ourselves
- Talent acquisition
- Heroic career
- Heroes making heroes
- The illusion of multitasking
- Failure and mistakes don't exist
- Discouraging change
- Hero invincibility

2. How do the heroes emphasize the selected effects?
3. Which effect is most prevalent in your company?
4. How has the most prevalent effect influenced your work?
5. Are there any other effects caused by your company's heroes?

IDENTIFYING THE TIPPING POINT

Remember my story about reaching the rock bottom of my heroic mindset and making someone cry? Here's the rest.

When I realized I'd overstepped, I apologized. But the damage was already done. I'd crossed a line and would reap the consequences. I felt horrible all weekend: I was stressed, overwhelmed, and disgusted with myself. That's when I began my transformation.

I cried.

I recall writing to my manager to explain the situation. I needed to report the incident. This was an acknowledgment that something wasn't working right. In my memory, something shifted that day. It was a point of no return. I was going to find another way to act, even if I had to do it alone.

I made up my mind.

For a long time, people had been advising me to leave the company. They said I should go somewhere else and stop tolerating this long-standing situation.

I was unhappy at work; it was a fact. It was obvious to me, if it happened in this company, it could happen in another.

If I didn't come up with a game plan on how to deal with it now, I was going to have to later.

I realized I had to act now. The following Monday, I still hadn't found any solution. But I had a clear idea: an unwavering desire to resolve this problem.

Because of this I was able to look at myself in the mirror and comprehend the extent of the problem. I was aware that people and my surroundings influenced my mindset.

The problem was bigger than me, and I wanted to understand it.

PRACTICE

I don't expect your story to be as emotionally charged as mine, to bring about change. In fact, I sincerely hope you haven't experienced or won't live through a similar situation. I've learned a lot from my actions, but they're not easily erased.

A friend often tells me, "You can hammer nails into a board, but when you take them out, the holes are still there." In other words, the damage is already done.

Whether you're the hero or surrounded by one or more heroes, this exercise will be helpful. You will be able to pinpoint why you want to change and validate whether the strategies in the next chapters will have the desired effect. Knowing you have a problem is the first step to change. Answer the following questions using sentences that begin with "I" (see the template available in the Resource section):

- Why do I want to understand the heroic mindset in the company where I work?
- Why do I want to change the heroic mindset around me or my own?
- What questions do I currently have that I'd like an answer to?
- What expectations or wishes do I have of this change?
- How do I currently feel about the heroic mindset?
- What kind of relationship do I want with my coworkers?

In the next chapter, we will look at strategies that can be used to counter the hero phenomenon.

CHAPTER 5
SIX STRATEGIES TO OUTWIT EVERYDAY HEROES

> Nothing is working!

My coworker at the time

When I got to the office and my coworker said that to me, the hero in me automatically turned on, and I was ready to face any situation. With extraordinarily little information from my coworker, a clear solution quickly popped into my mind.

I took control whether it was what my coworker wanted or not. I presumed that if I was asked for help, I would have to solve everything. If a coworker presented me with a problem on his screen, I'd take over his desk.

I always found the answers, but each time a new problem came up, I took over everything without explaining what I was doing. My coworkers didn't learn much and eventually came back with similar issues that I had to deal with time and time again. It was exasperating.

Working every day with one or more corporate heroes is

hard work. Employees pressured by heroes often don't know how to get out of the tricky situations described in the previous chapters. The following six strategies are useful for quickly solving many common business problems. They can be used individually or in combination. Try them now, and you'll see immediate effects on the heroes around you.

1. STOP SAYING "YES, BUT"

While reading the book *Coaching Agile Teams: A Companion for ScrumMasters, Agile Coaches, and Project Managers in Transition* by Lyssa Adkins (2010), I became aware of the number of times I was saying "yes, but" per minute. It was my typical way of answering almost anything, allowing me to insert my opinion into a conversation.

When someone uses "yes, but" to start a sentence, it automatically creates a conflict of ideas. The two people agree on one part, while disagreeing on other points which causes a debate. At first, there doesn't seem to be a problem, except that "yes, but" emphasizes the argument, dismissing the first part where they had initially agreed.

The "yes, buts" stack up one after another, and it's the last "yes, but" that is remembered. In other words, the basic idea is rejected, alongside others discussed. You go off on a tangent, and the point of the discussion is quickly forgotten. "Yes, but" statements don't include an idea, rather than exclude them. It's not a yes, it's not a no, it's a maybe and a way to dodge or sidestep. Most people try to avoid conflict, and "yes, but" is an easy way to achieve it.

Here's an example of a conversation where "yes, but" is predominant. The example is an interaction between two coworkers who always start with "yes, but."

"We should choose this training course for our employees, what do you think?"

- "Yes, but I saw that we already had a training course last month on a similar subject."
- "Yes, but this one is much more relevant to the new project we are starting."
- "Yes, but we don't have the budget."
- "Yes, but I thought it was in another budget."
- "Yes, but that was only for last year."
- "Yes, but the team won't have the necessary knowledge."
- "Yes, but I don't control the budget!"

In this example, two people constantly challenge each other, and you get the impression there's no end in sight until one of them gives in. The first sentence "We should choose this training for our employees, what do you think?" It was an invitation to give an opinion. However, each "yes, but" rejects the previous and the conversation becomes convoluted with each new round. The wording itself isn't bad, but when overused, it distracts the fellow speaker from the overall idea.

The first idea is quickly erased by the "yes, but." The conversation ends without answering the main question, "What do you think?" In addition, this conversation leaves a bad impression. The first person will no longer risk seeking the opinion of the second or anyone else. In this case, you think the training is not in the budget. What's the point in asking?

The hero is excellent at verbal jousting. He instantly connects ideas and finds a corresponding "yes, but" every time. He can also avoid all other possible phrasings of "yes, but" and jump straight to the last one. If we use the first sentence and the last "yes, but" we end up with a very lively interaction, "We should choose this training for our employees, don't you think?" "Yes, but I don't control the budget!" These kinds of responses make a healthy conversation between a coworker and the hero almost impossible. It increases the risk of misunderstanding. A simple request becomes difficult.

The hero uses "yes, but" for various reasons. As the expert, he defends his view and ensures all the details have been considered. He may be using "yes, but" to change the subject to avoid an uncomfortable conversation, or to steer the conversation and keep the focus of the coworkers on topics of interest rather than the original one. "Yes, but" allows the heroes to manipulate the conversation to their advantage.

Long "yes, but" statements cause similar deviations, and the corporate hero learns how to effectively use them. For example:

"Yes, I understand that the decision was made at the last meeting. I agree the stakes are complex, and we'll need to find innovative ways to get there, but we must understand we don't have a choice here."

Adding words between "yes" and "but" doesn't make the process any less manipulative. However, people notice it less.

Instead of saying "yes, but," say, "yes and."

The "yes and" indicates something more inclusive. The "yes" validates what you heard and your understanding of what has been discussed, and the "and" adds your own ideas. In this way, the two ideas are put together with equal footing. The "yes and" starts a discussion to generate something collaborative from these two ideas. The wording gives one of the two ideas the best alternative to use and shows acceptance of the idea.

- "I have an idea for the design of the document."
- "Yes, I've found examples in the files."
- "Yes, and I think we could do a layout."
- "Yes, and it could be used for another document."

- "Yes, and it would be a format that could be used throughout the company!"

Here we see how each idea builds upon the previous and creates a positive, inclusive conversation. It's a free-flowing conversation with no bad ideas. Both people are moving along the same line in hopes of creating something together.

The goal of "yes and" is to create clear language allowing team participation. It also prevents the hero from dominating the conversation. It's a simple strategy to use, which holds the biggest impact.

PRACTICE

- Use the template (see the Resource section) to count the number of times "yes, but" is said in a meeting. This will help you sharpen your listening skills and increase your awareness of this wording.
- Correct yourself when you say, "yes, but." Use the "yes and" formulation right away. It takes time to change this habit. It's helpful to start right away rather than wait for the next time.
- Focus on yourself and not others. Your efforts to change to a new habit help influence others and give you the opportunity to explain why you no longer use "yes, but."

2. SAY NO

I recall one team review in particular, the exact moment the team paused, observed themselves, and adjusted their way of working to improve. I was not the one in charge of the meeting, but I was there as an observer to provide guidance and feedback as needed.

The team wrote down several ideas for improvements on Post-its, and the facilitator read each of them. Some were simple, others were complex. I noticed that one idea dealt with a customer's changing requirements. The team struggled to manage the ad hoc changes that were always coming in and forced them to not reach their set deadline. The facilitator asked the team to be more flexible and accept the change despite the tight deadlines.

I felt uncomfortable with the facilitator's request; I'd previously experienced a similar situation. I raised my hand and said, "Do we have the right to say no?"

You could cut the tension in the room with a knife. I immediately saw the facilitator's face cringe. People froze in place and looked down. I had my answer, albeit silent, "No, never say no to a customer, even if the requests were unreasonable."

I'd asked the right question.

A real "no" is not a lack of collaboration. On the contrary, a "no" is a sign of transparency and honesty. It allows for a genuine debate on the subject in question. "No" highlights the differences between two ideas, whereas "yes, but" doesn't specify whether the other person agrees or not. You don't know whether the debate is open or closed.

Saying no is often perceived negatively as a lack of cooperation or a refusal to help. However, always saying yes can increase the risk of making mistakes. You need to spend more time justifying yourself.

I frequently work with teams where saying no is forbidden. "Yes, buts" are plentiful, but "Nos" are scarce. Often, people who said yes are willing to do anything to achieve the "yes." By saying yes, the person must achieve it, no matter the consequences. It's risky and harmful when the truth comes out. And it's impossible to honor obligations. The trust between coworkers is then broken.

"No" is a completely valid response.

It's not the sarcastic or disillusioned no of the Victim who says, "Oh no! Not again!" nor the implied no in "That's not what we said." It's a calm and clear no, a no that leaves no room for doubt. You know it's the right answer in this situation.

Taking no for an answer is a sign of professionalism, courage, and leadership. Saying no means being honest with yourself and the person you say it to. Saying it outright is difficult, especially to a supervisor. It's better to say it up front, steering the conversation to alternative solutions, rather than avoiding it with "yes, but." Moreover, "no" can be used very well with "yes and" to avoid "yes, but."

PRACTICE

- Remember: All questions or invitations can be answered with "No." Otherwise, they aren't real questions or invitations.
- Give people the right to say no by including it in your requests: "I can also take no for an answer." This will help people who fear to say, "No."
- Don't justify your "Nos." Resist the temptation to list all the reasons for your answer. Keep your answer short. Refer to the *Stop justifying* strategy below.

3. PUT AWAY THE DICTIONARY

The hero is an inescapable source of information, and people develop a reflex to consult him quickly. When a hero is asked a question, he answers. It quickly becomes clear that the same hero can answer any question. It's only a matter of time before the department, or even the whole company, asks the hero their questions. The hero becomes a living dictionary.

The problem is that the hero routinely answers. He provides the answers with no explanation on how to find the information. Coworkers learn which hero to use for which type of question they need answered. The overworked hero is interrupted with multiple questions, breaking his attention, and wasting valuable time switching from one task to another. What's more, the same questions are asked repeatedly, frustrating the hero. He replies, "I told you so the other day!"

PRACTICE PUTTING THE DICTIONARY AWAY

The first step is to avoid going to the hero with complaints such as "It doesn't work," "I don't understand anything," or "There's nothing that works." These are invitations to the hero to take the floor, giving more information than needed and limiting others' learning.

The second is to answer these three questions before consulting the hero:

1. What have I tried so far?
2. What do I understand about the situation?
3. What will I try next?

The first question asks about the current state of the situation. The answer is likely to be "nothing" if the habit is to go directly to the hero. The goal of this question is to learn to think on your own two feet and try something familiar before going to the hero.

The second question aims to stimulate reasoning by helping a person realize they may have a handle on the situation or at least part of the situation. Answering this question gives the inquirer confidence that he is also capable of figuring out things himself. You shouldn't ask yourself, "What don't I understand?" because it's impossible to explain what you don't understand. That's why a coworker asks for help in the first place.

The last question expresses the real topic of conversation to have with the hero. It's important to be straight to the point, to avoid sharing the whole thought process about the problem, and to keep the conversation short. It allows you to develop the ability to understand the problem on your own. You can approach the hero with a sentence like:

"I tried this and that, but it didn't work. I understand the system didn't receive the required information, but I don't know how to find out why. Where could I find the source of this problem?"

The hero also cycles through these three questions when general requests are asked. He does it swiftly, because he's used to thinking on his feet, especially when getting many complaints of "There's nothing that works!" By answering these three questions first, you're not asking the hero for help, and you may not need him the next time a question occurs.

The hero may give a long-winded explanation. You can either interrupt him by asking the original question, or just listen to him. It's best to return to the main question without getting lost, for greater efficiency. The goal is to stop seeing the hero as your only reference, after all. By practicing this mindset, the hero will be able to return to work quickly too.

PRACTICE PURPOSEFULLY GOING TO SEE SOMEONE ELSE

Another strategy related to Putting the Dictionary Away is not to ask the hero. This goes against our nature, as we know he'll have the answer in seconds. So why not? Here are a few valid reasons:

- Stop relying on one person, you won't be caught off guard when the hero is absent or unavailable. He's bound to be absent one day or another.
- Push yourself to develop a sense of self-reliance and find other ways to solve a problem.
- Enable other people to develop knowledge vital to the company.

Yes, it takes longer to get an answer. However, in the long-term teams acquire greater autonomy. Rather than banking exclusively on the hero's knowledge and speed, the company can rely on all its team members. The result means shorter response times and a reduced risk of losing the hero's knowledge if he leaves the company. The distribution of work within the team is also simplified, since it's no longer just the hero getting the job done.

4. WORK IN PAIRS

Working in pairs is a technique that's existed for many years. It's well documented in several books, such as *Extreme Programming Explained: Embrace Change* by Kent Beck and Cynthia Andres (2004), under the term "pair programming." The saying "Two heads are better than one" is well known. Working in pairs means interacting throughout the process, having real-time validation, and sharing knowledge on the fly. The result is better quality work.

However, this technique is not widely used in companies, under the argument that it is "time consuming." The belief is having two people work on the same thing, the cost is doubled! This statement is only true if we look at working in pairs from this angle alone. You also need to include all the activities involved. Whether you're working in pairs or not, you must ask your coworkers questions, get someone to validate your work, include the comments received, share your knowledge, and lastly complete the work.

Working separately creates delays between these different activities. Working in pairs seems to cost more. But adding up all the time associated with each individual step and the time waiting in between each, it becomes a win-win.

Another advantage of working with a coworker is less multitasking, as everyone is focused and switches less from one task to another. It's also a great bonding tool. You learn how to work together, manage a crisis, and broaden knowledge among team members.

PRACTICE

Working in pairs is simple: You need to decide a common goal and timeframe for completion and use the same computer or work area. The key factor is to complete the steps or tasks together and communicate throughout the process. Coworkers will then be able to share knowledge and validate their ideas on an ongoing basis.

Working in pairs with the hero can be intimidating, maybe pointless, if you're just sitting there not contributing. Here's a tip: Don't allow the hero to control the computer or pencil to avoid this situation. A coworker will learn faster if a hero hands over control to them. Just as in learning to drive, you need to take the wheel to develop your driving skills.

Another good practice for working in pairs is to give it time. Before you start, you and your coworker should establish a work timeline, even if you don't know how long it will take to complete a task. This allows an escape route from the overwhelming presence of the hero. Establishing a work time allows for breaks and you can learn the techniques without becoming tired. At the end of the set time, ask each other whether you want to continue or not.

It's important to mix and match coworkers. You get used to working with the same person and may be disappointed when they're unavailable. Better interaction is possible by changing pairs. Working in pairs also gives you the opportunity to learn with someone who has different skills than yours. The different perspectives each person contributes helps produce better results.

This technique can work with more than two people. However, it's best to master working in pairs first. Adding more team members too fast can become counterproductive, creating situations where only some are workers and others are watching. To integrate more than one coworker into pair working, it's best to draw inspiration from the Mob Programming approach ("Mob Programming" *Agile Alliance*, n.d.).

An example of a company that has introduced the concept of working in pairs on a large scale is Menlo Innovations, whose approach is well described in the book *Joy, Inc.: How We Built a Workplace People Love* by Richard Sheridan (2013). For this company, working in pairs is a fundamental practice. No employee works alone, and pairs are changed every few weeks to encourage interaction between employees.

Working in pairs is accessible to all and requires no special skills, which means you can begin experimenting right away.

5. INTERRUPT THE HERO

Understanding how to interrupt the hero avoids having to listen to his long-winded explanations or complaints. The goal is to stick to the point, not dodge it. The hero takes up all the space, especially when talking, whether at meetings, in the hall, or at the coffee machine. The instinct is to listen to the person speak until they finish, because that's what we've been taught. The hero can make the experience painful.

Interrupting someone is considered rude, yet it's a particularly useful strategy that can be done with good intentions. To do this, the important factor is the purpose, or objective, of the conversation in process with the hero. This purpose becomes your indicator of when you can interrupt. If the objective is to answer a question, and the question is answered, but the hero keeps on talking, that's a good indicator to interrupt. For example:"I needed this information, and you gave it to me. Can we continue our conversation next time?"

This is an example of an interruption. It's a reminder of the objective, followed by a closed question that can only be answered with a yes or no. In this way, we steer the conversation back on topic to avoid digressing, without upsetting the other person too much. An interruption always comes as a bit of a shock, and the aim is to soften it. The hero may want to continue talking despite the interruption. All you need to do is kindly repeat the same technique.

But above all, do it with kindness. Interruption should not be seen as a battle to be won against the hero. The hero acts the way he does because he's used to reacting this way. The goal is to break that habit so that both of you can be more effective. Looking at it as a battle against the hero is the best way to develop a Persecutor's position and perpetuate the problem.

PRACTICE

There is no perfect moment to interrupt the hero, but here are several tips:

- Wait for the moment when the hero stops to catch his breath between words. This moment is rather short, and you need to be on your toes to catch it.
- Raise your hand or your index finger to signal your wish to speak. This is an age-old trick that works well.
- Get physically closer to the hero. This will give you more opportunities to use the first two tricks. Getting closer to the camera during e-meetings also works.
- Do not speak louder or shout. The hero, like anyone else, will react poorly.
- Have a facilitator with a clear role in the meeting, who has permission to interrupt the conversation. People with this role are trained for these situations, as mentioned in the book *The Culture Game: Tools for the Agile Manager* by Daniel Mezick (2012).

Start by using just one trick. No matter what, it will tend to become the team norm, as your teammates will inevitably imitate you. Not only heroes need to be reminded that they're talking too much.

6. STOP JUSTIFYING YOURSELF

The title of the strategy says it all: People spend a lot of time justifying their actions so as not to cause trouble, make mistakes, or protect themselves. The result is often a long explanation to avoid being found out. The hero often uses it to serve his position. The more information he receives, the more he uses it to work the conversation to his advantage.

For example, when someone presents him with a decision and explains the whole story behind it, the hero can easily poke holes in it or criticize the reasons behind it because he wasn't present at the meeting.

It's not a matter of not explaining anything, but of not justifying yourself. Explaining is giving information to inform, understand, and clarify. Justifying is about convincing the other party and proving the decision or assertion is true. Justifying involves much more effort than explaining, since you're on the defensive. The defensive position makes you vulnerable, as you find yourself in a verbal joust with the hero, who exploits your weakness.

The hero thinks quickly: he excels at seeing things that are invisible to others. When faced with a decision or statement he doesn't like, his coworkers suffer criticism and emotional fallout. Justification gives the hero ammunition to abuse his position.

When he is a Persecutor, he uses the information received to target either the messenger or another coworker. He gathers information carefully, using it at the perfect moment to short-circuit a situation and take advantage of it. The more information he has, the more he has what it takes to manipulate conversations.

The Rescuer, on the other hand, benefits from the justifications of others because they justify his work. He uses them to explain his position as a Rescuer and to describe his achievements. For example, if he prevents the loss of an important customer at the last minute, all his coworkers must be informed of the circumstances, the new measures in place, and how he managed to avoid the worst. What should be an explanation becomes a justification.

For his part, the Victim uses the justifications of others to reinforce his position. He appropriates the problems and difficulties of others to enrich his storytelling arsenal. This ensures he always has something to complain about.

In every position, the hero loves gossip, rumor, hearsay, and other indirect information. He wants to know what's going on before anyone else and what's going on inside the company. He has a well-established network of coworkers to provide him with this information.

To outwit the hero daily, you need to stop feeding him more information than he needs. You need to provide a simple explanation or answer instead of a justification. The point is to reduce the amount of information he receives, not to break off or control all communication.

PRACTICE

- Avoid mass emails where you CC everyone you know, near or far. Reasons like "just in case he wants to know" or "so he'll know if anything goes wrong" are not good ones. They overload the inboxes of other employees, not just the heroes.
- Don't justify yourself immediately when a question is answerable by a simple yes or no. Wait until you're asked for clarification or an explanation. You'll be surprised how often you don't have to justify yourself.
- When the time comes to explain, keep your answer as short as possible. Get right to the point, without justifying each step.

There are hardly any times in business when you really must justify yourself. A question is not an interview, and a short answer more than meets most people's expectations. I, myself, am not immune to justification. A coworker gave me the best comment when he stopped me once in the middle of a justification, "You know, Dave, you don't have to justify yourself." He smiled at me and went on his way without waiting for the rest.

PATIENCE IS A VIRTUE

When I made the discussion to shed my heroic mindset, I had to practice patience to see results. I meticulously followed the strategies described in this chapter. I was used to hearing, "Nothing works!" I did not take the time to ask the right questions to get my coworkers to think like me and therefore stop thinking of me as their company's walking dictionary. One day, a coworker used the strategies himself.

He explained to me what he had tried and what he understood about a certain situation. When he said, "In your opinion, would it be better to apply solution 1 or solution 2?" I realized his dependence on me had ended. His reasoning was clear. He was coming to me for advice, not as a Rescuer. Finally, I felt relieved.

SUMMARY

It's important to know how to outwit heroes. You can reduce their disruptive behavior on those around you daily. Here are six easy strategies you can use at any time.

1. **Don't say "yes, but."** Instead, say, **"yes and."** "Yes and" builds on ideas. Also, it's inclusive, whereas "yes, but" puts forward an exception at the expense

of the main idea. Changing "yes, but" to "yes and" is the simplest and most effective strategy.

2. **Say no.** This allows you to be honest with the person and fosters a necessary debate. You need to have the guts to use it, rather than avoiding a debate. "No" is best used with "yes and" to avoid "yes, but."

3. **Put away the dictionary.** Corporate heroes are like a dictionary people use to get answers, rather than finding answers on their own. This increases dependency on heroes. Before you ask the hero, answer these three questions: 1) What have I tried so far? 2) What do I understand about the situation? 3) What will I try next?

4. **Work in pairs.** This is an easy way to share knowledge, validate your thinking with someone else, and increase quality of work. The cost of working in pairs is great in the short term, but it will outweigh the total cost associated with all the steps involved in working individually, also adding delays to the workflow.

5. **Interrupt the hero** to avoid both long-winded explanations and complaints.

6. **Stop justifying yourself** and limit the information the hero can use to reinforce his heroic position. Excessive information magnifies the phenomenon. Keeping your answers short and to the point helps outwit the hero.

These simple strategies can help outsmart the everyday hero, but shattering the hero culture in a company takes more than that. However, they are key to making an impact on the company, but you need to take the time to implement them.

Mastering them will give you the foundation needed for lasting change.

In the next chapter, we'll focus on the strategies that can be used across the board for your company. They go hand in hand with the six strategies we just explored, bringing a greater impact.

CHAPTER 6

HOW TO END HERO CULTURE WITHIN THE COMPANY

> An organization that designs a system, in the largest sense, will design a structure that is a copy of the organization's communication structure.

Melvin E. Conway

O ur companies grow more complex as they grow. Internal processes change to meet the employees' needs. Employees tend to juggle more and more options and features to develop in their job. This increase in complexity is normal. However, how we respond to its effects is what will foster the hero culture. These effects are then passed onto all levels within the company.

Conway's Law ("Conway's Law," 2023, December 22), by Melvin E. Conway, was first introduced in the 1960s to help explain the significance of a strong communication structure in a company and the mirror effect of this structure on the projects completed. Conway (1968) explains that not only does this phenomenon occur in projects, but also on different rungs of the corporate ladder. For example, a company's organization reflects the work completed by its teams. Similarly, the interaction between various committees, departments, decision-making heads, and work teams creates a complex structure of communication which is mirrored in the work performed.

The heroic mindset flourishes in professionals who try to adapt to their work environment to overcome challenges and achieve success. Based on Conway's Law, it is interesting to pose the following hypothesis:

"Is the phenomenon of hero culture in companies a reflection of the communication structure?"

To shatter the hero culture in companies, we need to change the way the communication structure works. It means transforming processes, groups, and their way of communicating ideas, objectives, and decisions throughout the company. This is what the next seven strategies suggest for influencing the hero culture.

1. REDUCE LARGE-SCALE MULTITASKING

Multitasking has been previously explained as a negative effect on the hero's availability and productivity. The hero's way of working has an impact on the company. Large-scale multitasking corresponds to the high number of projects or initiatives that a company undertakes at once across all its teams. To achieve this, *project portfolio management* covers the process involved in managing all activities. It's at this level that things must change to influence the hero culture.

Traditionally, we try to maximize overall productivity and employees' skills to finish all projects. This results in many projects competing for the same skilled people: the heroes.

Each of these projects requires a specific skill set. The company assigns the work to its best employees, the heroes, to successfully complete the projects in a timely manner. However, there are never enough heroes to handle all the projects. Even so, projects are greenlighted, the company wants quick results, and doesn't want to withdraw any projects from the workload. Heroes are continuously assigned one project after another to complete the goal set and deal with unexpected events.

The time lost in multitasking also occurs in the management of individual projects. Johanna Rothman (2016) describes the problem of large-scale simultaneous task performance nicely in her book *Manage Your Project Portfolio: Increase Your Capacity and Finish More Projects.*

Let's look at three projects to be completed, each estimated to last one month, and all depending on the same hero (see figure 6.1 below). The starting plan is for each project to be completed one after another, for a total duration of three months.

In fact, this does not represent the corporate hero's reality. Instead, he decides to start all three projects simultaneously. Other demands or unforeseen problems will only delay him. With project priorities changing during the process, the hero will justify the progress of the three projects. To keep up with the changes, he switches from one project to another, wasting precious time.

The reality is more like the second line (Actual). Not only is Project A not finished after one month, but it's taking longer to complete all three.

Figure 6.1—Planned vs. Actual

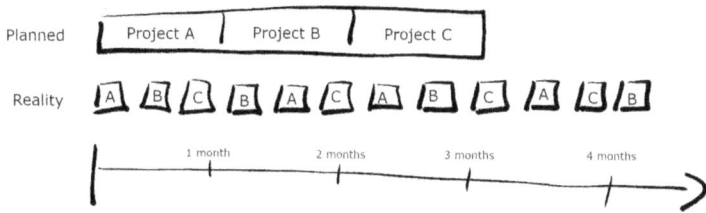

A company's portfolio may contain hundreds of ongoing projects. The time-wasting effect is multiplied by the number of projects and heroes involved. Full-time staff are needed to handle this headache. The plan must be constantly adjusted, and delays justified. Additionally, waivers are needed to justify added investments. And you need to deal with the dependence on heroes, one of the major sources of delays linked to multitasking.

Even if it seems counterintuitive or unusual for companies, we must reduce the number of simultaneous projects to achieve efficiency. The hero should not be assigned multiple projects at once. By reducing the number of ongoing projects, it decreases coordination effects and simplifies the communication structure. The fewer the interactions mean shorter delays due to multitasking and, ultimately, less reliance on heroes.

Employees find it difficult to say, "No, I'm not working on that project right now." However, this is the best response to meet deadlines and be efficient. It's not a hard "no," but rather indicates work won't begin anytime soon. In this way, you finish what you started before beginning something new. It's more satisfying and rewarding to finish one project than to juggle three at once.

The example of three one-month projects is rather rare. It's a more common practice for companies to manage projects over several months or years. The effect is even more pronounced, to the point of creating a serious management problem. Simply reducing project size will minimize the delays caused from multitasking. Dividing projects into smaller, more manageable tasks, instead of waiting until the end of the project and assigning all sub-tasks at once.

"Yes, but Dave, I have no choice but to..."
"That's all well and good, but I've always managed it that way."
"Yes, but the company would never want me to..."

If these sentences are on your mind, refer to the sections Stop saying "yes, but" and Say no in Chapter 5. This is a normal reaction, as it goes against the traditional way of managing projects in business. The following strategies offer additional practical solutions.

2. MOVE FROM INDIVIDUAL TO COLLECTIVE PLANNING

Planning employees' time is part of the normal day-to-day affairs in business. With heroes, this complex planning becomes more intense.

I've attended many time-planning meetings, and one left a real impression on me. It was a weekly meeting attended by a give or take a dozen project leaders and managers. The objective was to plan the work of each hero. By placing all requests for service down to the exact minute and following up weekly to ensure the plan is upheld. Here's an example of a plan that came from this meeting:

Table 6.1—Planning the Heroes' Work Schedule

	Project A	Project B	Project C	Project D	Project E	Total
Hero 1						
Hero 2						
Hero 3						

Several problems were evident:

- All the projects were run at the same time.
- The total time allotted per hero exceeded normal work hours per week.
- Unfinished work was carried over from one week to the next.
- The estimated time was unrealistic.
- Plan didn't count for the unforeseen events that heroes encounter weekly.

Participants' time in the meeting was poorly spent, and the plan would inevitably fail. The most incredible aspect was all the planning was done without any heroes' participation. In a discussion afterwards with the heroes, they expressed they wouldn't comply with the plan, since they don't consider it workable. This individual planning approach is focused on giving each person the optimal time to complete a project. However, we need to move from individual planning to collective planning, i.e., planning projects by work teams. The people in the right position to plan tasks are those who can complete them.

The Agile Movement Manifesto for Agile Software Development (Beck et al., 2001) strongly promotes this principle of team-based planning approach. The team plans the strategies, and the company manages the work without assigning it to individuals.

Collective planning stops coworkers from comparing themselves to each other, fosters team success, and ultimately eliminates the need for Rescuers to bear the brunt of every project. It reduces the reliance on "resource planning" committees. It empowers coworkers, and they create plans that take into consideration work capacity and reasonable deadlines.

> The whole is greater than the sum of its parts.
>
> *Aristotle*

Google set out to discover what makes its work teams effective. In their research, they found that understanding how a team works together matters more than understanding who the team members are (Google re: Work, Guide: Understand Team Effectiveness, n.d.). Effectiveness is therefore not due to the hero, but rather to the team's ability to collaborate.

FORGET THE WORD "RESOURCE"

A company's employees are not resources, tools, talents, or assets. These words are misleading and encourage a culture of heroes within the company, because too much significance is placed on their skills at the expense of their talents and traits. The word "resource" applies only to material, financial means, and or strategies. An employee is not a tool to be used and stored in a box when the job is completed. A person is more than a collection of talents. In staff recruiting, we hire the person, not the talent. Gil Broza (2015) discusses this matter at great length in his book *The Agile Mind-Set: Making Agile Processes Work, Chapter 4, People Are Not Resources.*

A collaborative approach with employees is essential. The

employee doesn't work *for* the company, but *with* the company. A partnership in which working together empowers the company and employee to achieve something greater than the sum of their parts. Changing words alters the perception of the relationship between the company and its employees. It's a company-wide "yes and."

Valuing the full individual potential of employees and relying on collective efficiency to achieve its objectives can significantly reduce the company's hero culture.

3. DIVERSIFY SKILLS

Experts are not the problem, but only having one expert for a specific skill puts companies at risk. Companies tend to specialize their employees, creating both dependency and scarcity. Employees are in danger of losing value and being replaced if their specialty is no longer needed in the market-place. Re-training in another specialty requires a great amount of effort and time, with no guarantee of success.

We should spare no expense in diversifying employee skills while promoting them. This allows heroes to stop relying solely on their specialty, and other employees can develop skills usually reserved for heroes. It is possible to diversify skills on several levels by:

- Setting up communities of practice to share knowledge between colleagues and encouraging discussions between experts and apprentices.
- Identifying the dependence and scarcity of skills in a work team
- Modifying employees' titles and job descriptions to be less specific about a skill.

The next sections explore these three ways of diversifying skills in work teams.

START COMMUNITIES OF PRACTICE

Communities of practice are self-organized workgroups focused on a topic of interest many employees have in common. The goal of the community is to share knowledge, feedback, and experiences, and to use that time to develop skills around a topic. It is possible to have training courses, invite guest speakers, test tools, host workshops and more. The form doesn't matter: the important thing is to promote the sharing of knowledge. Communities of practice have recurring scheduled meetings, with short periods of time between to keep their members engaged. However, the community of practice must determine its own operating parameters.

The time spent by employees in communities of practice should be included in their regular hours, not marked as personal time, since subjects discussed are related to work and conducted within the company. By doing this, more employees will be eager to participate, creating a ripple effect throughout the company. Additionally, it's a great way to let employees benefit from the know-how of outside consultants. By inviting them to this type of meeting, the conversation becomes even more relevant.

IDENTIFY SKILLS DEPENDENCY AND SCARCITY

Without a clear picture tool, it's difficult to get an overview of your team's skills and shortcomings. An easy way to accomplish this is to use the team competency matrix developed by the Management 3.0 group (n.d.). This is an exercise to be completed as a team, not just by the manager or the hero.

Figure 6.2—Team Competency Matrix

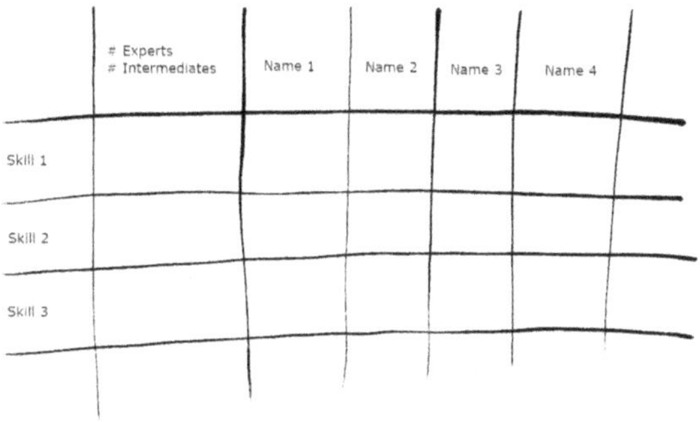

1. Use the template available online see (resource section) or draw a table where the rows are the skills, and the columns represent each person in the team see (figure 6.2).
2. Identify the team skills: tools, technologies, subjects, themes, processes, and practices, as well as non-technical skills such as listening.
3. Use the following categories: expert (I can teach it), intermediate (I can do it), and beginner (what is it?).
4. For each skill, determine how many team members are required to meet the team's needs. How many experts? How many with an intermediate level?
5. Ask each team member to do a self-assessed skills test, using the categories in point 3. If in doubt, choose an intermediate or beginner category to avoid overrating yourself and distorting the team's needs.

6. For each skill, check the difference between the total needed and the total skills the team currently possesses to identify where the gaps are and where sufficient effort has been done.

After completing the matrix, the team can brainstorm about what can be done to balance skills within the team. For example, the team has identified a skill which is needed by an expert, but no expert is on their team. The team can educate a team member using market-relevant training courses, pair with an expert, or recruit a new employee with the necessary skills.

With this exercise, the team can learn about each other's skills while coming up with a balanced plan. The plan will meet the needs of the entire team, not just the managers or the heroes. Completing the team competency matrix should be an interactive, easily accessible exercise that is updated at least a few times per year.

ADAPT JOB TITLES AND DESCRIPTIONS

Job titles and features are classically found within every company. They are highly visible and difficult to change. They identify employees' work roles and their status within the company. Job titles and descriptions are personalized, sometimes even unique, as they are based upon specialized skills. However, the more specific they are, the less room there is for the addition of newly acquired skills. The employee generally must change positions to have these skills recognized.

A good practice is to avoid naming tools, technologies, or other specific requirements in job titles, to allow the employees to diversify their skills outside the scope of their job description. In this way, the company is freed from having to recruit someone with the desired specialty. Also gone is the need to continuously update job titles and descriptions which can be quite tedious. The aim is to routinize the diversification of skills.

4. LET THE HERO GO

When working with the heroes is the norm, it's very difficult to let them go or replace them. The company avoids letting its heroes go, but when this happens, the team and the company are unbalanced, resulting to one of the following decisions:

- Hire an expert who can take over quickly.
- Transfer an expert from another team, though this creates a gap elsewhere.
- Appoint a team member as the new expert, which is like hailing a new hero.

In any case, these decisions don't solve the problem of dependency and scarcity. It's only a matter of time before the same thing happens again.

I remember when a hero had just left the company where I worked. My team was at a loss; everyone was wondering how they could help clients with situations that only the hero had ever dealt with. Our team leader asked us: "From 1 to 10, what is the level of risk associated with this departure?" The team replied: "11!" No one could replace the hero. Still, it was the best thing that ever happened to the team. We didn't want to experience the stress of being helpless in an unknown situation again. The team decided to learn the missing skills without appointing a new hero.

Let's look at how to let the hero go for good.

First, **don't replace the hero.** Use this opportunity to develop the missing skills within the team. Instead of preparing to replace the hero, we should establish a game plan to tackle any gap within the existing team.

Whether he is on vacation or sick leave, replacing the hero is a recurring challenge. This situation should be communicated to the team as a learning experience that will avoid recreating a precarious situation in the future. Please, do not say, "We are not planning on replacing the person. We'll have to make do without them." This statement can weaken work teams. A better way to say it is: "We're not planning to replace the person. We'll find another way to learn the missing skills as a team."

We need to **call upon another expert colleague to train the team in its missing skills.** It's not a question of hiring someone to act as a new hero, nor of robbing another team of its experts. We use another colleague to reestablish the skill level of the team members for a brief period as they return to their own work groups. If your company decides to recruit a new employee anyway, he or she should not be assigned the role of the hero in the team. This person should complement the others, not replace the hero who left.

If the hero remains uncooperative despite the efforts made by team members, managers, and others, the hero must be removed. This step is only possible if the company values the diversification of skills and believes in developing its employees' potential.

Taking the hero out of his comfort zone is risky because he loses his "expert" status. His reaction may be to develop a new heroic attitude in the new team. This type of change must be done with a clear set of objectives to help the hero grow. The company should also actively support him in this change. A hero whose role within the company was forcibly changed can seem defensive and reluctant to learn. A good tactic is to try a time-limited experiment to minimize the hero's resistance to change. It could be an experiment for the team too, who will no longer have their expert with them. Changing the hero's place in the company can benefit both the team and the hero, as the team learns to work without relying on the hero's skills.

If all else fails, consider firing the hero. Sometimes it is the only solution, especially when the hero has more of a negative impact than a positive one on the company, teams and employees, and any attempt to make a change won't temper his heroic attitude. Companies usually have a clear set of rules on how and why to dismiss employees, and they should be followed. Dismissal may be difficult to accept, but we wouldn't want to be left with an untouchable employee or an *invincible hero* as we saw in chapter 3.

Heroes are a short-term solution, and by letting them go, we leverage the whole team in the long run.

5. LIMIT OVERTIME

Heroes are likely to work overtime, and this causes other employees to work overtime too. It's not uncommon for heroes to be online extremely late, or to see them on the second day with a solution they developed the night before by working outside normal working hours.

This overtime is often not even recorded. The company may promote and normalize this practice, which in turn drives a wedge between the heroes and the other employees, while overworking the entire workforce. Burnout, stress, and anxiety ensue, possibly leading to even more severe psychological disorders. There is a Japanese word for people who die from working too much: "karoshi" ("Karoshi," 2023, May 10). In Japan, the work culture values overtime. Thus, the hero creates a standard in the team where extra hours are necessary.

Overtime should be the last resort option. It shouldn't be

seen as a solution to meet commitments, i.e., meeting a project delivery date or completing a task more quickly. Here are a few tips to help you avoid standardizing overtime:

- Don't schedule all your available work time. Remain flexible by freeing up some time. You'll be able to then deal with the unexpected without having to work overtime.
- Disconnect all devices from the company's network when you are away from the office. Unless you're on call, there's no need to be connected.
- Define clear rules about overtime and make them accessible to everyone in the company.

Overtime comes with the belief that you always must do more and that you never have enough time to finish everything. Companies are constantly trying to outdo each other, we see this year after year, and the expectations of employees are rising too. The heroes see overtime as a solution to achieve this. The hero writes the rules and leads by example. Therefore, it is in the company's best interest to proactively manage their allotment of overtime.

6. MAKE INTERNAL COMMUNICATION TRANSPARENT

There are many channels through which information is communicated within a company: email, announcements, team meeting, file sharing, informal discussions, telephone calls, video conferences, posters on the wall, etc. All these channels are good if they are used at the right time and are visible to the people concerned. Unfortunately, these two conditions are difficult to meet, and the company must make additional efforts to address any shortcomings.

One of the reasons why this happens is that information is only available to an elite group for as long as it takes to craft the right message. This group learns the information first and eventually the other employees are informed. The problem in this model is the time lapse between the new formatted information and when the employees receive it.

Persecutors and Rescuers are a part of this elite group. They have access to privileged information before anyone else. The victim hero, on the other hand, has delayed access to information. They often complain that the company has poor communication management. This exclusive access to information feeds the rumor mill and fosters feelings of mistrust, especially when we start hearing employees say, "They aren't telling us the whole story." Basically, in the informal network, information is obtained more quickly than in a formal network.

These common corporate practices underpin the problem that information flows at two different rates:

- Friday 3 p.m. email with hard-to-accept news. This is a tactic to avoid confrontation and postpone interaction until Monday.
- Vague communications containing non-specific information. This type of communication clearly states that there *is* information to disclose, but the elite group feels it's too early to share with the employees because it hasn't been vetted. Employees then feel they cannot be trusted and complain.
- The information is shared by a third party who doesn't have any power over the content of the message. This method allows information to be

shared quickly within a company, but it prevents employees from getting straight answers to their questions, since the messenger has as little information as anyone else's.

- Detailed information is provided several days or even weeks after the initial announcement. When employees receive information at the last minute, they feel excluded from the change that is taking place. They will be inclined to resist rather than accept the message. Employees are presented with a mission accomplished, and it's too late to address their concerns.

Employees want to be included in the change and receive the same information as everybody. We should include them early in the communication process and communicate freely what we do *and* do not know yet. Pretending to be in control of everything is simply unrealistic. Employees are suspicious of a perfectly crafted message in which all the issues are played down. They suspect this is just the tip of the iceberg, regardless.

Transparency is the key to curbing the hero culture. If everyone has the same information, heroes no longer have the upper hand. Only a small amount of information is truly confidential. It's controlled by limited accessibility from designated employees. Other information we try to withhold eventually leaks through the informal communication network.

Rather than letting information leak out without knowing who knows what and when, the company should promptly keep its employees informed. Employees can voice their concerns faster when there is a steady flow of information, which in turn stops feeding the rumor mill. We are not trying to silence the informal network: we are making it our ally.

Here are a handful of transparent practices to maximize the exchange of information:

- Hold frequent and recurring information opportunities. Seek employees' input to determine the right frequency.
- Vary communication channels to maximize the reach. Word-of-mouth is one of the best ways to reach many employees. However, using multiple channels at once is a better way.
- Repeat information more than once, since it's unlikely to reach everyone at the same time, especially in a bigger company.
- Avoid the question, "Do you have any issues or questions?" this is a closed question and doesn't allow people to speak up. A better way to ask is, "What questions do you have?" This allows for open-ended conversation, which cannot be dismissed by staying quiet.

We should reduce the distance between the source and the recipients. Conway's law states that reducing the number of people involved simplifies the communication structure. In our case, we stop feeding the hero culture.

7. ENCOURAGE CONTINUOUS IMPROVEMENT

> Dave, you have to understand that…

Just another day manager

These words always stopped me dead in my tracks as I was trying to suggest an idea for improvements. I wasn't given a "no" or even a "yes, but." However, it felt like the rug was pulled out from under me before I could say or do anything. Therefore, I scratched my ideas for improvement. This strengthened my victim hero position, by putting up with my misery. I would have liked to be listened to and encouraged to test my ideas.

Continuous improvement is essential in companies so that they can adapt to change. Today, change happens more frequently, and companies need to improve rapidly to prevent competition from taking the lead.

However, humans don't like change. We accept change if it concerns others, not ourselves. Continuous improvement and innovation are not possible in the company until the company takes deliberate action.

To shatter the hero culture within a company, we need to question the current ways of doing things. Change can be achieved by understanding how it can impact us, and by gradually integrating it into our work with purpose. Experimentation is also needed to support learning among coworkers and improving practices.

A good experiment is framed with clear guidelines. It's not just about trying something to "see what happens." Often, employees avoid experimentation because they see it as a waste of time and there are chances it won't work out as expected. Often, employees don't know how to express their expectations properly and their managers won't allot time for experimentation.

An easy way to experiment is to use the PDCA (Plan, Do, Check, Act) method ("PDCA," 2023, April 17) developed by Walter A. Shewhart, and more commonly known through William Edwards Deming's work. It consists of four stages:

1. Plan the experiment

- Formulate a hypothesis. This is a question you are trying to confirm or refute. It takes the form of a clear statement whose conclusion is currently unknown.
- Plan the actions you want to take to test a hypothesis.
- Use the following statement of purpose: "If I do [insert action here], I think it will cause [insert expectation here], and I'll be able to validate it if [insert success condition here].

2. Experiment

- Use a set time for the experiment. It needs a beginning and an end.

3. Observe and verify results

- Once the actions are completed, it's time to observe the effects.
- Use the following questions: Did we obtain the expected results? Have the conditions for success been met? Did anything unexpected happen?

4. Decide your next steps

- Decide how to use the results.
- Use these questions: What did we learn? Did we succeed in confirming our hypothesis? Should we adapt the next experiment? Should we call it a day?

We must complete these four stages in our experiment to

benefit from the results. It doesn't come with a guarantee for success. If we knew the results in advance, the experiment would fail, and ultimately be a waste of time. There is always some risk, possibilities to make mistakes, therefore missing the boat on the expected outcome. And this is where companies often give up on experiments. They just don't want to waste time. They are only willing to try what works, so they won't have to justify time loss.

But there is some good news! Experiments are *not* a waste of time, because you are learning. Even if you don't get the expected results, experimentation allows you to act rather than just think about hypotheses for improvement.

During experimentation, you can mitigate some of the risk by controlling the time allotted to carry out the intended work. It's better to do a short experiment to learn the process than do nothing at all. At the very least, you will learn something. As you get more familiar with experimentation, your risk tolerance increases as well. You need time to learn.

To foster continuous improvement and innovation, the company must:

- Allow for mistakes, or rather, give people opportunities to learn.
- Establish specific guidelines for experimentation and communicate them clearly to the staff.
- Accept that every good practice is the best practice until a better one is found. All good practices are temporary.
- Treat experimentation as work: it is done during normal working hours and valued the same as other tasks.

Continuous improvement can be supported by experimentation and challenge the ways of doing things that maintain the hero culture. The company also empowers all employees to streamline their workday without having to constantly rely on the heroes.

SUMMARY

Based on Conway's Law, the culture phenomenon of heroes in the workplace reflects the structure of the internal communication within the company. To shatter the hero culture throughout the organization, we need to change the ways of doing things that drive the phenomenon. Here are the seven strategies examined in this chapter:

1. **Reduce multitasking on a large scale** to limit the number and size of simultaneous projects to achieve efficiency. The demand for heroes decreases when multitasking is reduced.
2. **Move from individual planning to collective planning** to reduce the risk of employees comparing themselves. It encourages teamwork and brings success to the team.
3. **Diversify skills** within the work team to reduce dependence on a single hero, who provides the necessary knowledge to carry out the work.
4. **Let the hero go** is a better solution than trying to replace him.
5. **Limit Overtime** to avoid overwork. Overtime should only be used as a last resort.
6. **Make internal communications transparent** to include employees earlier in the effort to put a stop to rumors and misunderstanding. The informal communication network becomes an ally, not a threat.

7. **Encourage continuous improvement**. The company must support experimentation. To encourage employees to experiment, they must be allowed to make mistakes and receive a clear set of guidelines. Experimentation must be treated as work, to encourage employee participation.

Strategies applied at the corporate level require a more significant change in how things are done. They must be used jointly with those provided to outsmart the heroes every single day. It's a difficult change to make because several business methods have been drilled for years and thus have become second nature. Later chapters will touch on methods to tackle large-scale culture change.

We still need to look at the hero's perspective. The next chapter will focus on the strategies to use when *we* are the hero.

CHAPTER 7
WHEN I'M THE HERO

Since I took off during the summer vacations, I had to prepare the team and my customers several weeks in advance. I spent days noting down the details I had kept to myself about our current projects using the request tracking system. The workday before my vacation started, I imagined all sorts of disaster scenarios. I saw panic written all over my coworkers' faces as well.

When I got back from my leave, I had 983 emails, and my voicemail was full. Handwritten notes were all over my desk, and my coworkers came in to tell me everything that had happened while I was off. My manager dropped by shortly after, saying, "I hope you got some rest! We need to talk. I've got an emergency for you." The emergency was a request pending for weeks because it was easier to wait for me to return than to complete it themselves. I was exhausted before lunchtime and spent the following three weeks making up for lost time.

Every year was the same and after several years, I wondered, "Why am I even taking a vacation? It would be easier not to take any."

That same year, I realized *I* was the hero at work. I had come to believe that taking a vacation was too complicated, that I was the only one who knew critical details about the work to be completed. I complained every time something unexpected happened, and I started treating my coworkers badly. I thought I was stuck in a job that would be gone in a few years.

At first, I was scared, and I ran away from the situation. I didn't want to be the type of coworker with an ugly attitude. It took a strong will to decide to act. I was embarrassed about treating my coworkers badly, and I truly didn't want to ask them for help. In fact, I didn't think anyone could help me or understand the tricky situation I was facing.

I set out on my own to change my attitude.

Today, I wouldn't make the same mistake. I'd call on my network of coworkers and friends for moral support.

It took me nearly three years to change my attitude on my own. I couldn't make sense of my difficulties or easily find solutions to fix my relationship with my coworkers. I did a lot of trial and error before finding a strategy that worked. In hindsight, I should've asked for professional help to be heard and get to know myself better. I'm glad I learned how to grow from this experience. I hope that the heroes out there won't keep quiet about their struggles.

Being a hero is an attitude in response to an environment. The attitude doesn't define the person. More importantly, no one should feel bad for realizing they are a hero. The remaining parts of this chapter require a healthy dose of self-esteem. It's never too late to learn and grow.

TURBOCHARGED STRATEGIES FOR THE HERO AMONG US

The strategies presented in the previous chapters are useful for both employees and managers. However, they need to be adapted slightly for the hero. These strategies can change the hero's attitude while influencing others who struggle working alongside them.

Most people don't want the hero to stop being a hero, because he is key to a smooth-running machine for the team. Still, the hero can change the work dynamic with his team by using the strategies suited for him. And for better results, include those around you. Not everyone is lucky enough to read this book!

Instead of going over the strategies again, let's look at how they differ from the hero's perspective. If you're unsure, refer to Chapters 4 and 5 for full details on each tactic.

1. STOP SAYING "YES, BUT"

"Yes, but" is a double-edged sword. On one hand, the hero uses it to make his point, and on the other, ensures that no detail is overlooked. The "yes, and" has the power to both include and invite other people's ideas, which allows for collaboration among coworkers, rather than taking part in a joust to see who gets the final say.

It's hard to resist the urge to say "yes, but." It takes both practice and patience not to cave in and use it. Here are a few tips on how to change this habit:

- Repeat the following sentence three times before each meeting: "I'm going to say 'yes, and' instead of 'yes, but'." For best results, say the sentence aloud or write it down.

- Listen to understand rather than to answer. "Yes, but" flows naturally because they are constantly used to respond to others. If we try to understand what others say, the new response will be to build on ideas with the "yes, and."
- Pay attention to the other's use of "yes, but" to avoid triggering a "yes, but" as an answer. Those who work with the hero are used to saying "yes, but" so they can win any argument with him.
- Make a short pause before answering. Count to three to allow yourself time to say "yes, and" rather than "yes, but."
- Be resilient and give yourself time to change the "yes, but" habit. After a few weeks, it will get easier.

"Yes, but" encourages coworkers and the hero to argue, whereas the "yes, and" makes the hero an outstanding collaborator. Changing the language, the hero uses trains other coworkers to collaborate rather than argue, because he is a role model in the company.

2. SAY NO

The hero's "no" is powerful. It's difficult for coworkers to compete with the hero's "no." As the expert, the hero has all the arguments needed to justify his stance. To encourage openness and inclusiveness it's best to reduce the use of "no" and opt for "yes, and."

It's a good idea to add a brief explanation to clarify the reason for a "no" to avoid discouraging coworkers. This way, no one will feel like the hero isn't listening or simply asserting his authority.

"No" is a sharper answer than a "yes, but" and avoids the domino effect of "yes, but."

3. PUT THE DICTIONARY AWAY

Employees can learn problem-solving skills with this tactic, without any help from the hero. Plus, the hero can benefit from it too. He can learn how to change the dynamic when coworkers use him as a walking dictionary.

Whenever "Nothing's working!" it's important to take a break. You *must* hold back from replying. Instead, use the following three questions with a coworker in that order:

1. What have you tried so far?
2. What do you understand about the situation?
3. What will you try next?

The hero guides the coworker to each question without giving away the answers. If they can't answer them, he can offer choices. For example, the hero asks:

"What are you going to try next?"

"I don't know! I have no idea!"

"Perhaps you could check the documentation. Or call the team manager and ask them?"

"Good idea, I hadn't thought of that."

The hero should never do the work for the coworker. The goal is to let them learn for themselves, so that they can find the best way to do it without your help.

The hero also is also responsible for guiding his coworkers. Letting someone search for hours for an answer can snowball into major consequences for customer service or possibly have serious financial consequences for the company. Luckily, the hero can judge how long is too long to let a coworker find a solution because of his experience and his expertise. Several factors can guide the hero in making this judgment call, such as how urgent the problem is, the level of service required for the customer, how risky it is to extend the response time, or what their coworkers' skill level is.

Using this approach, the hero can avoid leaving coworkers searching unnecessarily for too long, while developing their problem-solving skills. If a coworker comes up with an emergency, it's not the right time to ask those three questions. First, address the emergency with the person, guide them through the steps involved in resolving the situation, instead of solving the problem for them. We can explain the solutions once the emergency is over. Our goal is to encourage learning, not to do completely without the hero.

4. WORK IN PAIRS

This tactic is an opportunity to share the hero's knowledge with others. The most important thing is for the hero to work in a pair with everyone on the team. He should not play favorites with one or two coworkers by solely focusing his attention on them.

It can be intimidating for coworkers to work in a pair with a hero. The hero should take the initiative to invite other team members to work with him. Alternatively, if the hero is in high demand, this is a great time for two coworkers to learn to work together, while having the hero as a sounding board for questions. When this occurs and the pair seeks help, the hero applies the dictionary tactic by asking the three questions to promote problem-solving thinking.

The hero can also deliberately choose who to work with to get the most positive impact. For example, he may choose to work with the coworker who knows the least about the subject, to give them the most attention and the knowledge they need to become independent.

In any case, the hero shouldn't be the one running the computer to support learning. If the need arises, he or she should give back control to the other person as soon as possible.

The hero needs to avoid spending his whole day working in pairs. He must set aside time to accomplish tasks only he can complete. A good practice is to set a 45 to 90-minute time slot and let the team know.

5. INTERRUPT THE HERO

The hero not only relies on the ability of other colleagues to interrupt him but can also learn to limit his spoken interventions and leave the floor to his colleagues. This is a form of self-interruption. Here are some tips to achieve this:

- Ensure that meetings have a clear objective. If not, propose one to limit the scope of the meeting and avoid diverging conversations. The hero will realize that his topic is irrelevant or not on topic.
- Talk for less time. According to *Neuro Learning* (Gil, Medjad et al. Lacroix, 2016, p. 83), attention drops dramatically at the ten-minute mark. The hero must give the floor to others when the time is up.
- Limit the amount of information you give. Don't overload a coworker with all your knowledge every time a question is asked. Keep this passion

for communities of practice or other moments conducive to long exchanges like debates.

- Stop yourself and ask if enough information was provided. After a brief explanation, the hero can ask: "Is this enough information, or do I need to say more?"

Interrupting oneself requires more listening skills and discipline than interrupting others. However, it encourages coworkers to participate and shows them that it's acceptable to interrupt the hero.

6. STOP JUSTIFYING YOURSELF

The hero justifies himself when he tries to convince others or to prove that his decision or assertion is true. It's a defense mechanism. He wants to make sure that his ideas are accepted, and that there is no room left to negotiate.

By justifying himself, the hero quickly discourages others, because he has a thorough understanding of his expertise that allows him to easily play with details and nuances. Successfully disproving a hero is no easy task, nor does it allow for ease of collaboration with him.

To stop justifying oneself goes hand in hand with the previous tactic, where the hero interrupts himself. The goal is to leave more room for discussion and constructive debate. Thus, the positions of Persecutor, Rescuer, and Victim occupy less room in the conversation.

Do these three things instead of justifying yourself:

- Explain
- Simplify
- Summarize

The hero must learn to say less while staying relevant.

7. REDUCE MULTITASKING MODE

For the hero, reducing the number of tasks performed simultaneously is not an easy feat. The nature of his work means constantly shifting from one task to another. It's unrealistic to think a hero can work on only one task at a time. However, there are ways to reduce multitasking and certainly not to increase them.

The first way is to reduce the number of activities in progress. Here are some options:

1. Use the tactic *Say No* to avoid automatically accepting new activities. You can complete your tasks before turning your attention to new ones.
2. Replace one activity with another when you can't say no. Try to remove an activity from the existing list. Prioritize on your own or ask for a manager to do so and remove or postpone an activity. This is a great way to limit multitasking.
3. Ask for a later delivery date, rather than the desired date. One way a hero accepts more and more activities is by asking: "When do you need this by? The answer is typically: "ASAP," so he becomes inevitably overwhelmed. Instead, ask: "How long can you wait until I send it to you?" The hero can then better plan the order in which to complete the activities instead of jumping from one task to another.
4. Establish clear rules for prioritizing work. Without them, all requests become urgent, and who shouts the loudest gets his requests done first. The best way to accomplish this is to have a top ten list of

key activities to do and one activity for each item on the list. The rules set *must* be strict and sub-priorities shouldn't be used (1.1, 1.2, 1.3, or even 0!) which basically short-circuits the list.

The second way is to take an active role in long-term planning of future projects, instead of allowing coworkers to decide themselves. The hero can split long projects into shorter smaller ones, without compromising their success. This is difficult for coworkers who lack the experience. Jeff Patton's Story Mapping (n.d.) is an excellent way of doing this.

Story Mapping allows the user to visualize all the activities of a user journey and map our understanding of the work to be done for a given project. The technique consists of five steps:

1. **Frame:** You explain the purpose of the project, what the benefits are, and why it's important. For example, you define the intention of a book and who is the target audience.
2. **Map the big picture:** You write down all the major tasks in a summary form, like the table of contents in a book that explains the book's journey. The goal is to see the whole picture, not just parts of it.
3. **Explore:** You describe in detail each of the major tasks from the prior step. The sky's the limit. For example, you write down all the content you want to add to a book, questions to be answered, exercises to be completed, references, etc.
4. **Break down viable versions:** Since it's impossible to do everything at once, you need to segment the work into self-contained sections. For example, a

first digital version of a book is made available, then a second print version, and finally a third version would be to have an audiobook. In all cases, each version can be used with all the necessary sections, rather than the author trying to make a chapter usable for all three versions at the same time.

5. **Determine an implementation strategy:** You split the work that needs to be done for the first version of the previous step. For example, you break down the work needed to complete the digital version of a book.

Story mapping provides an overview of the entire project, mapping the work to be completed all the way to the customer experience. Viable versions are used to limit the scope of the work to a more targeted objective, rather than trying to do all the tasks of the project at once.

8. MOVE FROM INDIVIDUAL TO COLLECTIVE PLANNING

The hero can perform tasks alone, but he must voluntarily change this approach to minimize dependence on his expertise. There are several tips about that in the *Working in Pair* section of this chapter. However, there is still an important point about planning team activities that needs to be pointed out.

The hero tends to estimate the time needed based on his ability and his own speed. Trying to plan tasks according to each member separately will result in a different estimated time needed from one coworker to another. This is even more the case for the hero. A good practice is to plan according to the average capacity of the team, excluding the hero. For example, if he can finish in one day, but the team needs three, use a three-day schedule.

The hero must avoid making promises on behalf of his team based on his own capacity, as explained by Mark Burgess (2015) in his book *Thinking in the Promises: Designing Systems for Cooperation*. This prevents the company from making unrealistic expectations. Besides, they must manage overrun costs and deadlines when promises are not respected. The hero's first instinct should be to estimate the work as if someone else was doing it for them. Or even better, invite the team in the estimation of the project. Expectations will be more reliable. If the hero will be carrying out the task, the client would be able to enjoy a better turnaround time than what was originally planned.

9. DIVERSIFY SKILLS

The hero is the ideal candidate to initiate a community of practice around his field of expertise. He has a platform to share his knowledge and help diversify the skills of his coworkers. He can manage the learning sequence for a given skill to improve effectiveness, which will in turn help coworkers save time on less relevant subjects.

The hero will often receive new knowledge first. Coworkers rarely have access to specialized training, conferences, seminars before he does. For a coworker to diversify their skills, the hero must make room for them to learn something new. A good way to achieve this is by rotating staff who will take part in professional development events. The whole team can then benefit from this while the company can reduce its dependency on the hero who is not trained on this new knowledge.

The hero must learn to delegate. We often hear him say that it takes longer to explain than do it himself. In the short term, it's true: the hero *will* be faster. However, in the long term, our dependency on him grows while he becomes less and less available.

The problem is that we see work as an indivisible whole, not as a series of small tasks. A coworker with few skills can do some of the work. The hero can delegate some tasks to coworkers who can carry them out. That leaves him with the parts the team can't accomplish.

The goal is to involve coworkers in the work that only heroes can perform from the beginning. Delegating certain tasks reduces the hero's workload, thereby reducing multi-tasking.

10. LET THE HERO GO

The best way to relinquish your role as a hero is to become irrelevant. Allowing the team to take ownership of its specific knowledge and skills makes it easier for the hero to leave the company. The hero can switch to another position or another company without the pressure of staying on or burdening the team with too much stress.

When I decided to leave, my manager asked the team, "From one to ten, what is the level of risk following his departure?" My manager thought I was still the Rescuer he needed. The team replied, "Two." There was close to no risk, since I'd spent the last two years making myself useless and training the whole team. My departure went off without a hitch.

By being aware of the impact a hero has on the company, they can give notice of leaving and make a transition plan accordingly. The change is smoother when both the hero and the company work together on this. However, the company may be hesitant to let the hero go and will use various strategies to avoid it by offering a pay raise, a new title, more responsibilities, or possibly even making the hero feel guilty for wanting to leave. In all cases, this only delays the inevitable: the hero *will* leave.

11. LIMIT OVERTIME

I remember my first job: I was both passionate and motivated by the work. It got to the point where I'd log onto my computer at night to keep working, even though I couldn't bill for the unauthorized overtime.

Working in the evening eventually became a habit driven by obligation. This was the only way to complete the project on time or clear my weekly task list. Since those weren't billable hours, they didn't register in the company's statistics, and thus the company wrongly assumed I could do more and more.

The truth is, I was always doing above and beyond, but at my own expense. I wasn't paid for my extra hours *and* my personal time suffered from it.

When the hero manages to complete more and more tasks, the company assumes the hero's limits haven't been reached yet. The hero must learn how to say no to overtime: first, to not sacrifice his personal time for work, and secondly, to force the company to find other solutions. Even if overtime is paid, the harmful effects remain.

Overtime must remain the exception to the rule. Discussing what happened in different venues is recommended when overtime is frequent or used by default. Employees are the best people to inform the company that overtime has become a problem. The conversation must take place with all parties concerned to bring effective and fair solutions.

12. MAKE INTERNAL COMMUNICATIONS TRANSPARENT

The hero must contribute to internal communications. With his expertise and experience, he has privileged access to information. His first reaction should be to share the information, rather than keep it for himself. The continuous sharing of information will prevent coworkers from asking directly for it.

If the company supports transparency, the hero won't feel remorse or be penalized for divulging information. On the other hand, if the company wishes to inform only the hero, specifically asking not to repeat anything, we must find another way to inform the coworkers.

A former manager had a simple way of sharing information he couldn't divulge. He would take a risk by telling us but would make us responsible for not repeating anything. He would organize an impromptu meeting and say: "What's said here stays here, but everyone will leave the room with the same information." A coworker could have spilled the beans anytime, but still, it fostered a sense of trust. The whole team received the information simultaneously, so there was no need for anyone to ask questions on the sly. In all the years I worked with this manager, I never witnessed a coworker break this trust.

It's in the hero's interest to share information with those around him to encourage trust and accountability and to avoid spreading rumors.

13. ENCOURAGE CONTINUOUS IMPROVEMENT

Opportunities for continuous improvement are easy to use for the hero. He is in the right position to propose ideas and lead improvement initiatives. He can also help explain the potential gains to justify the investment in time.

When the hero has ideas on how to improve the way things are done, he must communicate it and involve his coworkers in the process. For example, he could ask a coworker to work in pairs.

If the idea comes from a coworker, the hero must avoid discouraging their initiative, even if their proposed idea is not the best. The key is to encourage them by accepting their ideas alongside those of the hero. The hero can then judge whether the idea has potential to help or harm and suggest adjustments if needed.

The third question in the *Put Away the Dictionary* tactic is, "What are you going to try next?" This question launches an ongoing improvement process depending on the answer. The hero can then help plan and participate in activities with his coworkers.

Continuous improvement initiatives don't need to be large-scale corporate projects. Smaller initiatives are easier to take on, because they are more accessible to all employees on a regular basis. They will have a better chance of being completed, as they compete with the number of ongoing activities in the company.

The hero should avoid making improvements on his own at all costs. In other words, he must involve his colleagues and become a "team player."

SOME STRATEGIES TAILORED TO THE HERO

All the strategies described below are useful for colleagues working with a hero. However, they are presented primarily for the hero himself.

1. STOP OUTDOING YOURSELF

When I first started working, I was eager to acquire new knowledge. I invested a lot of time reading blogs on software development, subscribing to all the newsletters on the sites I visited, and downloading everything I could on software development best practices. I also bought books on current best practices, listened to a lot of Ted conferences, took part in knowledge sharing events, paid for online training, and so on. I soon realized that I needed to acquire new knowledge to be able to do a good job and continue to develop my skills. It was also necessary to advance to other, more prestigious, and lucrative positions. I couldn't help but add each accomplishment in my email signature with a series of acronyms corresponding to the certifications I'd achieved.

At first, it was fun and rewarding to go hunting for information and acquire new skills. But there's no end to this type of self-improvement. We're overwhelmed by a nagging feeling that we'll never have enough knowledge to be fully competent, or that without this certification or that course, we'll never be "good enough".

In his book, *The Elegant Self: A Radical Approach to Personal Evolution for Greater Influence in Life*, Rob McNamara (2013) talks about the state of mind in which a person is constantly seeking self-approval through seeking more knowledge without appreciating how far they've come in their learning. As if acquiring more and more knowledge could give you a strong enough sense of accomplishment to finally allow you to relax. Rob McNamara goes on to say that the need to outdo oneself is an incentive for humans to develop, but that eventually, this need becomes impossible to fulfill, which limits us in our development.

The hero wants to be good at everything and is continually striving to improve. He thinks he's not good enough.

This feeling is called impostor syndrome ("Impostor Syndrome", December 19, 2023). It means you're constantly doubting your abilities. Our hero quickly takes on a self-improvement project, which fuels his over-specialization.

Our shortcomings are opportunities to benefit from the expertise of others. Instead of becoming a master of all, the hero can connect with coworkers who are better at things than him. It's not a question of highlighting his weaknesses, but his ability to work as a team member, and to accept help. And of course, to realize that other people can be very competent too.

- Stop pushing yourself too hard by not over-consuming information and knowledge.

For example, it's better to take one or two relevant training courses throughout the year, apply and build upon newly acquired knowledge before looking for a new course. You want to avoid the equivalent of binge-watching series of streaming platforms, where you're constantly looking for a new series to watch. You need to take a break between series to enjoy another. You should also limit the list of certifications to add to your name to one or two relevant ones in your LinkedIn profile or electronic signature. You will be focusing less on your achievements and your coworkers will like you more.

- Reduce the number of subscriptions to newsletters or magazines you signed up for, especially those you never read.

Better yet: unsubscribe from the ones you haven't read in a while. Clean up emails so you do not miss newsletters that really interest you. Don't hesitate to cancel a subscription and resubscribe later if needed. Both taste and information change constantly and so do our sources.

- Read the books you have readily available on your desk or shelves.

For example, books you bought because they pique your interest at the time of purchase but haven't read because you didn't have time. The same goes with those hundreds of unread emails we should read. In any case, it's best to save time for reading on a regular basis and avoid building a long list of reading materials that can discourage you. Books can be either offered or lent to a coworker. Emails are only relevant for a few weeks, so it's better to delete them and stop being afraid of missing out on something we haven't read.

2. ASK FOR HELP

My mother used to say, "You can't help someone who doesn't want to be helped." In coaching, this saying is especially true, because without my client's consent to help them, they'll suffer from my help. Our relationship will be strained because my client will be too focused on defending his point of view, rather than accepting my advice.

Asking for help is difficult for the hero because it implies becoming vulnerable. This vulnerability is uncomfortable for him. He must admit that he is incapable of doing something and that may make him look incompetent.

Brené Brown (2010) explains in her TED talk "The Power of Vulnerability" that being vulnerable helps create bonds of trust. We need to show courage by sharing facts about ourselves, show compassion for ourselves and others, and seek a connection with those around us, to create a sense of belonging. Vulnerability translates into actions such as trying something with no assurance of success, giving negative feedback to someone, or sending someone away. But also acknowledge your mistakes, being transparent about projects not going according to plan, or answering "No" to the question, "Are you okay?"

Vulnerable actions make us authentic and real in the eyes of our coworkers. We stop pretending everything is fine and that there's no problem. It's in the best interest of the hero to develop this quality, to make himself more accessible, and allowing for open communication with coworkers for help.

3. ASK MORE QUESTIONS

Asking questions leaves room for an open discussion. The strategies *Stop saying "yes, but"* and *say "no"* are effective in this sense. The hero shouldn't assume he understands what his coworkers means, or else he risks misinterpreting their intentions. It's also a good way to open a discussion and exchange ideas. For example:

"What do you mean, it's all over?"
"What does (insert work or concept here) mean to you?"
"Why are you interested in learning this skill?"

By taking an interest in his coworkers with questions, the hero invites them to participate. It's a way of encouraging exchange and use the skills learned in this chapter.

REDUCING MY HERO FOOTPRINT.

Throughout the years, these strategies have helped me to make room for my coworkers. I remember times when I held back from adding a comment or a "yes, but." I was particularly proud when I attended a meeting and left without saying a word! I didn't need to attend. At last, I had proof that I could turn down invitations, since my coworkers could keep going without me on occasion.

The personal work I've done using the strategies discussed in this chapter has enabled me to appreciate the work of my coworkers, acknowledge their skills, and integrate their ideas. I learned to make room for them by highlighting their successes and referring to their expertise when someone needed help. By loosening my hero's grip on the team, I allowed its members to develop without undermining my own value. In fact, taking up less space gave me unique opportunities to accompany several teams on their journey.

SUMMARY

The strategies discussed in chapters 4 and 5 must be adapted to the hero's perspective.

1. **Stop saying "yes, but"** is an exercise that needs to be deliberately practiced to be assimilated. If the hero does it, others will.
2. **Say no** quickly cuts off the conversation. It's better to say "yes and."
3. **Put away the dictionary** is a tactic that works best when the hero uses it himself.
4. **Work in pairs** allows the hero to share his knowledge. He must leave control of the computer to his coworker to maximize learning.
5. **Interrupt the hero** works even better when the hero learns to interrupt himself.
6. **Stop the hero from justifying himself** allows him to make more room for his coworkers. It's better to explain, shorten, and simplify.

7. **Reduce multitasking** is necessary, both in the terms of the number of activities performed by the hero, and with the hero's active participation in reducing multitasking for the company.

8. **Shifting from individual to collective planning,** pushes the hero to estimate work according to the team's speed, not his own.

9. **Diversify skills** is an activity that the hero can encourage in the company. He must also learn to delegate tasks that his coworkers can do.

10. **Let the hero go** means the hero tries to make himself useless. By helping his team improve their skills, he can ensure an easier transition.

11. **Limit overtime** to situations that truly require it. The hero must learn to say no and help the company find better ways.

12. **Make internal communications transparent** requires the hero's participation, due to his privileged access to information.

13. **Encourage continuous improvement** is put forward by the hero, who can help his coworkers and the company. It's a good idea to build on short improvement initiatives and make sure they are finished.

Three other strategies are specific to the hero's perspective:

1. **Do not outdo yourself** all the time, by constantly seeking new knowledge and skills, which gives the impression of never being good enough. The hero's shortcomings are opportunities to invite others to collaborate and benefit from their expertise.

2. **Ask for help** is not a weakness, but a strength, allowing the hero to become closer to his coworkers.

3. **Ask more questions** helps to avoid taking for granted that the hero understands what his coworker means.

Now that we've seen all the strategies, let's see which ones to choose first. The next chapter offers informed choices for each heroic position, at company level and among the immediate circle of the hero.

CHAPTER 8
PICK THE RIGHT STRATEGIES

“ Yeah, but what am I supposed to do now?

An attendee at one of my conferences about heroes

After three chapters detailing various strategies, it's time to consolidate what you've learned and work out how to put them into practice at your workplace. Some strategies are easier than others to implement in your daily work.

There's no point in using all the strategies at once. Even if they are complementary, it is worthwhile to introduce them gradually to avoid wasting your efforts.

Since these strategies are used differently among each type of individual, chapters 5, 6, and 7 are categorized according to these perspectives:

- Chapter 5 offers strategies for workers who work with one or more heroes daily. This is the hero's inner circle.

- Chapter 6 looks at the executive levels in the company and proposes strategies that affect processes and how tasks are completed. These strategies can be applied on a small scale before applying them to the whole company.
- Chapter 7 offers strategies for the hero.

In this chapter, we'll investigate strategies to start transforming your workplace.

FOR THE HERO'S INNER CIRCLE

The first strategy to integrate into daily practice is to stop saying "yes, but" and replace it with "yes and." It has a positive impact on team collaboration and its effect is immediate, since "yes and" is an invitation to collaborate instead of a way of avoiding it.

Before we change all the "yes, buts" at once, it's important to listen and identify how often "yes, but" is used in our everyday language. It appears in formal conversations like a team meeting, or informal conversations like a discussion about our weekends around the water cooler. The trick is to pick them out of the conversations and get used to hearing "yes, but." The template for counting "yes, buts" found in Chapter 5 (Resource section) is a good tool to help you.

Once you've begun to recognize the "yes, but", you can then practice changing it to "yes, and." Information and knowledge-sharing meetings, or informal discussions around the coffee machine are excellent places to begin your practice. It's easier to remember to use "yes and" once you express them naturally in informal conversations. The next step is to integrate "yes and" into formal conversations like a team meeting for instance.

The more you practice every day, the more natural "yes and" will become.

A sign "yes and" is becoming easier is when others' use of "yes, but" becomes annoying to you. However, you must resist the urge to correct your coworkers on the spot. It's best to stay focused and practice to avoid disrupting the meeting by explaining why you have to say "yes and."

Another trick is to talk to coworkers close to you with whom communication is easy. Together, the "yes and" will have a ripple down effect on the others.

Saying "no" is a strategy that can help you in the same way as saying "yes, but." It may take a few weeks or months to get comfortable using these two strategies. "Yes, but" is ingrained in our language, and it's completely normal not to be successful in the first few days.

Working in Pairs and *Putting the Dictionary Away* strategies will require more planning. Working in pairs is done by scheduling joint working time with either a coworker or the hero. Scheduling time is preferable, rather than proposing it out of the blue. If this is a new tactic for you or your coworkers, it's best to work in pairs for a short time. Personally, I prefer to schedule between 45 and 90 minutes. Less than 45 minutes is hard for a good pair dynamic with productive outcomes. Planning a 90-minute session is useful for longer tasks, but fatigue can set in beyond the 90-minute window. It's easier to schedule short sessions, rather than none, when everyone's schedules are full.

To successfully put the dictionary away, it's important to have clear concise thoughts before talking to the hero. The goal is to avoid rushing to him with questions. It's best to have the following three questions on hand:

1. What have I tried so far?
2. What do I understand about the situation?

3. What will I try next?

Put the three questions on a Post-it, on your phone or in a notebook, so they are readily available. If mentally answering the questions is complicated, then write down your answers before you rush to see the hero. Answering these questions are for you and not a way to avoid the conversation. The goal is to improve communication and develop a stronger working relationship with the hero, not to cut ties with him.

The last two strategies are applied asynchronously. *Interrupt the hero* and *stop justifying yourself* will be useful from time to time. They can't be planned, which means they should be used when the time arises.

We often think about using these two strategies after the fact, for example, after a meeting where the hero gave a long presentation. In this example, it would be better to interrupt the hero, rather than let him talk too long.

Here are some tricks introduced in Chapter 5 for interrupting the hero:

- Interrupt the hero when he catches his breath
- Raise your hand
- Get closer physically
- Avoid speaking loudly or shouting
- Delegate the role of a facilitator in the meeting to manage the right to speak

Thinking back on prior conversations where we had to justify ourselves, tell yourself you'll do better next time with the following:

- Avoid mass emailing everyone using the BCC feature

- Wait until someone asks for an explanation before giving one
- Keep replies short

Strategies for the hero's immediate environment improve collaboration with not only the hero, but other coworkers. They have the potential to become the new best practices in communication and collaboration at work.

FOR THE COMPANY

Business strategies should be used gradually. They are not designed to be adopted company-wide instantaneously. Radical change would cause resistance from the workers.

The steps for large-scale changes are explained throughout Chapter 10. To start, it's best to focus on a team within the company who is open to improving, without undertaking a large-scale process.

The most important strategy to prioritize is to *encourage continuous improvement*, which we discussed in Chapter 6. This tactic may be already in place, but it's a great stepping-stone to introduce all the other strategies. Prioritizing time for continuous improvement allows company executives to redefine workflows, one step at a time.

More often, the main issue is time needed to invest in changing the way things are done. If prioritizing time for continuous improvement is an issue, it's easier to focus on small improvement lasting a few hours. Communicating the results learned through the improvement initiatives is important. The main objective is to eventually greenlight further actions that will result in making continuous improvement a standard practice.

If continuous improvement is already a common practice, then the other strategies will be more easily integrated. Here are a few suggestions for improvement with the other strategies to ensure a smooth integration:

Plan the implementation of (name of strategy)

1. Introduce an initial action to start using this strategy.
2. Implement another action to take the strategy a step further.

Reduce multitasking on a large scale

1. Clearly show the number of simultaneous tasks for each member to raise awareness. Include current, pending, and blocked tasks.
2. Decide as a team the maximum number of tasks one can have at the same time, so the hero doesn't have to do everything at once.

Move from individual to collective planning

1. Prioritizes tasks instead of planning the hero's work. He can provide his own list of achievements for the week.
2. Do your estimates as a team, rather than having the hero doing them. Team estimates are more realistic for everyone and not just for the hero.

Diversify skills

1. Plan working in pairs as discussed in the *For the Hero's Inner Circle* section in this chapter.
2. Complete a team competency matrix as described in Chapter 6, section 3 called *Diversifying skills*. The

matrix will help the teams working together to address specialization issues.

Let the Hero Go

1. When the hero exits the team, it's important for the remaining team members to discuss the best way to solve problems that will arise. The goal is resisting the gut instinct to replace him without discussing first.
2. Use the team competency matrix to identify the missing skills without the hero. Make a game plan to develop each skill within the team. Only look for a replacement for skills the team members cannot develop on their own.

Limit Overtime

1. Avoid planning 100 percent of the available time. Plan 80 percent which leaves room for unforeseen circumstances. To fill the remaining 20 percent, the team should have a list of priorities on hand.
2. Turn off company notifications outside normal work hours. You can turn them off directly on your phone over a set period.

Make Internal Communications Transparent

1. Establish a weekly routine to share current news and gather questions. Conducting short 15-to-30-minute meeting is a start in the right direction, to avoid disrupting other people's schedules too much.

2. At weekly meetings, invite whichever coworker is in the best position in the company to give updates.

FOR THE HERO

Use all the strategies discussed in Chapter 7 with a few variations from the hero's point of view. Select a strategy and put it into practice each week. It will help curb negative effects like the hero being the only source of information, being unavailable, or being over-specialized.

Most importantly, his coworkers and the company must reduce their dependency on him. The strategies in Chapter 7 focus on this specific point but applying them depends on each hero's position: Persecutor, Rescuer, or Victim. Once you have mastered those strategies, the rest can be integrated one at a time, in no particular order.

PERSECUTOR

To stop saying "yes, but" is the preferred strategy because it is mainly responsible for rejecting the ideas other coworkers propose. By shifting to "yes and", the persecutor becomes more approachable. You can accomplish this by using the tricks discussed in this chapter's section for the hero's inner circle and learn to transform "yes, but" into "yes and."

A second strategy to use from the beginning is to reduce multitasking. It helps reduce the bottleneck effect, in which, the number of tasks requiring the hero's attention is greater than his ability to complete them.

A third strategy is the Pomodoro technique developed by Francesco Cirillo (n.d.). It allows to maximize your focus and limit interruptions to take full advantage of the time available. Each "pomodoro" consists of working time and break time. By avoiding long sessions, you avoid mental fatigue and minimize the risk of being interrupted by your coworkers. Here are the 5 steps of the Pomodoro technique:

1. Choose a task
2. Set a timer for 25 minutes
3. Work on task until the timer goes off
4. Take a short 5-minute break
5. After every four "pomodoro" take a longer break

Stop saying "yes, but" and *Reduce multitasking* will quickly help the persecutor positively change his relationship with his coworkers.

RESCUER

The *Putting away the dictionary* strategy has an immediate effect on the team's dependency on the hero's knowledge. It helps reduce general issues like when people say that "nothing works" and it forces coworkers to think on their own and develop problem-solving skills. Therefore, the hero becomes less indispensable, and coworkers are better prepared. You can help your coworkers achieve this is with these 3 questions in the following order:

1. What have you done so far?
2. What do you understand about the situation?
3. What will you try next?

Working in pairs is also a good strategy to start with right from the get-go. It spares one person from having to do all the work, plus it helps diversify the team's skills. Your coworkers become learners, who put into practice their knowledge by participating directly in the task at hand. The hero can schedule short periods of pair work when carrying out tasks he knows he has expertise in. Or he can simply ask informally, "Is anyone on the team available to work on this task with me?"

With the strategies *Putting Away the Dictionary* and *Working in Pairs*, the Rescuer reduces dependency by helping coworkers develop their own skills.

VICTIM

The key factor of the victim is to minimize the feeling of being victimized. A good starting point is to use the *Stop justifying yourself* strategy. Justification begins when the hero tries to convince his coworkers that he is right or when he is trying to protect himself. Instead of justifying himself, the hero should:

- Explain the situation with facts
- Use short answers
- Wait to be asked, rather than automatically explain

A second strategy to use from the start is to *Encourage continuous improvement*. The victim is often in this position because a situation is complicating their work, and he cannot find a way to resolve it. He focuses their energy on fixing what is bothering them. Complex situations can be difficult to deal with, but every little improvement is worthwhile. The goal is to start improving continuously so it becomes natural with practice. The hero becomes involved in the change, rather than having the rescuer do it for him.

1. Plan the necessary improvement by selecting an issue which needs to be fixed and decide on one or two specific actions. A good example is to facilitate a retrospective workshop, like Esther Derby and Diana Larsen recommend in their book *Agile*

Retrospectives: Making Good Teams Great (Pragmatic Programmers) (2006).

2. Perform planned actions, preferably with coworkers.

3. Observe and verify results to confirm that actions have produced expected results.

4. Decide what to do next, either continuing with another action or stopping. Communicate the results to coworkers.

The main barrier to continuous improvement is that the victim feels "nothing is really going to change." This is due to the complexity of the problem they're trying to solve. Additionally, they can't change the parameters necessary. Improvement initiatives work best when broken down into smaller actions, focusing first on elements you can control and take it from there, one step at a time.

Both strategies *Stop justifying yourself* and *encourage continuous improvement* go hand in hand in helping the victim learn to stop thinking they are constantly the victim in the workplace.

The first strategies are the most difficult to use. When they are regularly practiced, they take less effort to use each time. The important thing is to be resilient and continue. If in doubt, refer to your answers from Chapter 4, and pay special attention to this question: "Why do I want to change the heroic attitude around me or at home?"

The next chapter explains new positions that can replace the Persecutor, Rescuer, and the Victim. Together, they create a new culture that does not depend on heroes.

CHAPTER 9
REINVENTING THE HEROIC ATTITUDE

> No matter what our job title says, the goal is to solve the customer's problem.

A Coworker

I remember a powerful moment when we were three coworkers from competing companies who shared the same client. There was a problem that required all our different skill sets to solve. We set aside our titles, and our corporate names to focus on a common goal. One of us could have been a persecutor or Rescuer to one up the others, or another one of us could have taken the role of the victim by telling the other team members to deal with *their* problem.

We adopted positions that were collaborative and positive to face the problem head on as a team. I was proud to call them coworkers, even though we were all working for different companies at the time.

In this chapter, we take a deep dive into new concepts to help us understand the positive attitude we can develop beyond the hero. It is based on how to address the problems at hand and which step of a business lifecycle your company is. Three new positions can replace the persecutor, rescuer, and victim. These will be briefly described in this chapter to give your insight on how to transform our heroes. Later in the book, we will discuss this at greater lengths.

CHANGING THE PERSPECTIVE REGARDING THE PROBLEMS

But first, there is an important point to make about how the hero perceives problems.

We often hear the hero complain, saying things like, "Why does this always happen to me?", "Luck's never been on my side", "These things only happen to me." The hero sees problems as situations that fall on his lap, with this overwhelming feeling that something will go wrong, and that always specifically target him. The hero sees problems or obstacles as a threat.

The hero fears these threats will materialize and goes into reactive mode. The minute he catches his breath, the cycle repeats with a new problem.

The hero reacts defensively, developing a strong dislike of change. Even when improving the situation is possible, his instinct is to resist for fear of causing a problem. When I suggested an improvement, my manager used to say to me, "We'll see when it doesn't work anymore. For now, let's leave it alone."

The change in perspective occurs when the problems or obstacles become opportunities to participate, to make a difference, rather than a situation to discard.

While unpredictable, these opportunities facilitate learning and collaboration with coworkers. The hero is inquisitive about the question on hand and won't be taking a defensive stance. He shifts from being reactive to becoming creative when tackling a problem. William A. Adams and Robert J. Anderson (2106) introduce this concept on perspective shift in their book *Mastering Leadership: An Integrated Framework for Breaking through Performance and Extraordinary Business Results* as a cornerstone in transforming leadership style.

Figure 9.1—Shifting Perspective on Problems

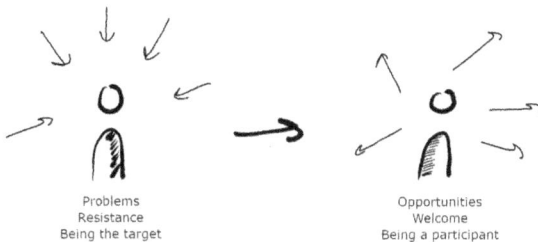

Problems
Resistance
Being the target

Opportunities
Welcome
Being a participant

This change of perspective is essential to the hero's transformation, as he no longer resists the fact that problems do and will occur. By ending this resistance, the hero deals with situations as they come up with an open mind, which helps him develop the three new positions that follow.

THE *CHALLENGER—COACH—CREATOR* DYNAMIC

The three positions of Karpman's Drama Triangle (Persecutor, Rescuer, Victim) that explain the hero can be transformed into new, more creative, positions. David Emerald (2013) presents them in his book, The Power of TED* (*The Empowerment Dynamic*), as a new dynamic triangle. The old position finds its equivalent in the new positive dynamic. These positions now serve to create a corporate culture where negative effects of heroes (see Chapters 2 and 3) are greatly minimized.

Figure 9.2—Reactive to Creative Positions

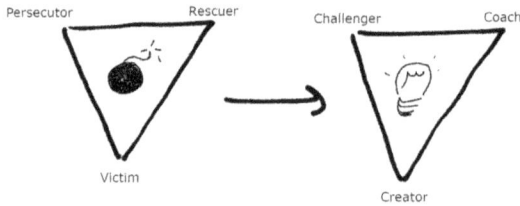

The next sections explain the new positions: Challenger, Coach, and Creator and how they differ from the previous positions: Persecutor, Rescuer, and Victim. These new positions come with new reactions that are supported by the strategies in Chapters 5 and 7.

When the hero masters these new positions, he can let go of the need to be a full-time hero. In fact, the hero label doesn't apply to these new positions. They allow the hero to adopt a new role, which marks a turning point in his attitude, as noted in *The 4 Ways of Leading* (n.d.) published by The Conscious Leadership Group.

Please note that these new positions are not exclusively for heroes but they can be developed with the whole staff within your company. It is not necessary to develop all these new positions at the same time. They are meant to change a reactive attitude into a creative attitude, one position at a time. As a hero, however, you should develop a creative position that best defines you. For example, a Rescuer might first focus on the coaching position, before incorporating the other two.

FROM PERSECUTOR TO CHALLENGER

Rather than criticize, the challenger has an uplifting attitude and bonds easily with coworkers. The challenger is bold and doesn't hesitate to speak their mind. They ask the questions no one else dares to. They also possess a clear vision and defend it tooth and nail. They can explain their vision skillfully which inspires their coworker to follow them.

My client said to me once: "You've got to coach this expert. My employees can't stand working with him, but I must keep him on the team." I wasn't sure how to approach this professional coaching since the expert in question was a persecutor who didn't want my help. Instead of trying to change him, I decided to ask him for help, so he could become a challenger. By asking his opinion, including him in the coaching, the expert developed his challenger position. He then applied this new position to his own work. Shortly thereafter, the employees were comfortable collaborating with him on other topics.

The challenger can inspire those around him. He's the type of mentor employees want; he dedicates his time to helping others learn and grow. Coworkers deliberately plan their schedules to work with the challenger, because they know it will be transformative. The challenger doesn't blink twice on passing on his knowledge. Coworkers say things like, "I absolutely want to work with you. I've asked to be assigned to the same project so we could work together."

Team members appreciate whenever the challenger can take part in team meetings because he brings new ideas. The challenger supports his coworkers and his resilience to problems is contagious. Whenever he shares his opinion, his comments are constructive and aligned with the team's objectives. He is truly invested in his work, which is key to bring about change.

The challenger welcomes mistakes because he sees them as a learning opportunity. He may even go as far as to prompt mistakes to promote faster learning. For him, reliability can be found in how you can effectively bounce back after making a mistake, learn from this, and choose to never give up. He doesn't waste valuable time trying to foresee every worst-case scenario. He understands that things may not go according to plan, but that he can count on his resilience to adapt.

Table 9.1—Characteristics of the persecutor-versus-challenger

Persecutor	Challenger
Imposes his vision	Inspires
Feels entitled to everything	Encourages
Keeps work to himself	Acts as a mentor
Takes other people's place	Demonstrates resilience
Prevents others from taking their place	Reassures
Resists change	Is a leader
Avoids failure	Brings innovative ideas
Doesn't like to accept help	Promotes learning
Overturns decisions	Encourages you to work with him
Disrupts	Is spoken of in a positive light
Blames	
Is more often spoken of in negative than positive terms	

FROM RESCUER TO COACH

Being in a Coach position inspires others to seek growth. The coach can see the coworkers in their best light and supports them in their growth and learning. His ability to listen and his curiosity makes him a reliable person. He's easy to confide in and trust completely.

A client approached me with the following request, "I'm tired of being the Rescuer, but I don't know what else to do." After several conversations with this client, we found a balance between being the expert for the company without the work teams constantly depending on his knowledge. He made sure his coworkers had the necessary knowledge and delegated as many tasks as possible on the team's shoulders, so he wouldn't be the focus of every conversation. He increasingly adopted a Coach position, rather than the Rescuer or expert.

The Coach's advice is always welcome because he doesn't force his opinion on people, even when he knows the answers to the problems. He shares his experience to bring his own perspective without overshadowing others. In fact, he can easily invite his coworkers' point of view and ensure everyone will be heard. He knows how to make himself available to have the greatest impact.

The Coach leaves plenty of room for coworkers. He is patient in his explanations and repeats himself willingly. His goal is to make coworkers autonomous and less dependent on him. Coaches enjoy seeing their coworkers succeed. Team success is on the coach's mind, not individual success.

Questions are the coach's best tool. He asks questions to provoke thoughtful answers and allow coworkers to learn to think on their own two feet. He doesn't ask questions to avoid answering them, but to foster learning by letting coworkers perform the actions.

When emergencies occur, the coach is levelheaded, which means he won't panic and will remain calm. He helps his coworkers break down the urgent situation into small, clear steps and guides them through each step. The unknown and the unpredictable are not sources of stress for the Coach; he's confident, even without knowing all the steps of a plan beforehand.

Table 9.2–Characteristics of Rescuer versus Coach

Rescuer	Coach
Creates a dependence on his skills	Active listener
Seeks recognition and visibility	Is curious
Imposes his presence	Has humility
Is always ready before others	Makes others grow
Keeps knowledge for himself	Is inclusive
Benefits from a protection against mistakes	Inspires trust
Is indispensable in too many projects at once	Reassures
Is rarely available when necessary	Support
	Advises
	Guides

FROM VICTIM TO CREATOR

The Creator is a positive force, who brings solutions to problems, rather than criticize. She usually has ideas her coworkers hadn't considered. Her coworkers will say, "Good thing you're here!" Or "We'd never have thought of doing it that way!" This new position focuses on innovation, continuous improvement, and change.

I coached the member of a team who had an annoying habit of criticizing the efforts by whispering to another coworker during team meetings, "It doesn't work" and "It won't work if you do it like that" or "I've seen it done better elsewhere." He usually left meetings without expressing his ideas. I decided to stop seeing him as a person who only complained and rarely shared his ideas to the team. I called on him in the middle of a meeting so he could speak up. I focused on his ideas for improvements, rather than the criticisms. After a few meetings, the plan worked. He was listened to, he no longer hesitated to put forward his ideas, and he became an essential source of improvement for the team.

Working with a Creator brings happiness to the job. There's nothing she can't handle, even the most complex problems don't seem to faze or discourage her. She often has multiple solutions to the problem, she is willing to test her hypothesis, and she involves her coworkers in the process. The Creator has several tools in her belt to promote collaboration. Coworkers ask often ask her what the best tool is to solve unfamiliar problems.

The Creator is ready to help at a moment's notice. She is fully committed to whatever role the company needs. Her positive impact shines when she participates in all stages of achieving change, from idea to implementation.

As a great communicator, she doesn't hesitate to share the information she has with her coworkers. She has a down-to-earth attitude, therefore her plan for solving a problem includes both the pros and the cons without having any preconceived ideas.

Table 9.3—Characteristics of Victim Versus Creator

Victim	Creator
Has trouble saying no	Communicates easily
Complains	Brings innovative ideas
Criticizes without bringing solutions	Supports continuous improvement
Puts the blame on others	Is positive
Is trapped in his role	Shows commitment
Is pessimistic	Perceives problems as challenges
Contributes to rumors	Is fearless
Monopolizes attention	

The new creative positions of Challenger, Coach, and Creator are accessible to everyone within the company. There's no reason to develop the reactive positions of Persecutor, Rescuer, and Victim before drawing inspiration from them. In fact, it's better to adopt creative positions in the workplace now, before the negative effects of reactive positions take hold.

An overview of the Challenger, Coach, and Creator positions helps to visualize what the hero can become by changing his attitude. However, developing them requires some personal investment and support from the company. This subject will be addressed in a future book on transforming hero culture. However, reading David Emerald's book, *The Power of TED* (*The Empowerment Dynamic), is a good starting point for those who want to learn more now.

AN EXAMPLE OF APPLYING THE CHALLENGER-COACH-CREATOR POSITIONS

I used to act as a link between the production team and the client. Essentially, I was an analyst, I clarified the customer's needs and passed them on to the team. After the team completed the job, I checked whether the customer was satisfied, and their needs were met. The steps were simple but applying them was complex. A major problem often occurred where the customer was unsatisfied, and his needs were indeed not met.

The first instinct was to blame the team, though it was not the case. The team members were professional with high quality work—that was not the problem. The other instinct was to blame the customer, by saying it was their fault for not asking for the right thing. How could we read their mind? But this was *my* job, I spent hours gathering needs and passing them to the team. Was *I* the problem after all?

It was at this point that the change of perspective took place.

With my Persecutor-Rescuer-Victim positions, I would have jumped at the chance to place the blame on the team and customer, and then defend myself by saying there was nothing I could do about it. Instead, I used the Challenger-Coach-Creator positions to find out the real reason, test a solution, deploy it, and make it the team's new best practice.

As I investigated, I discovered that there was a misunderstanding between the customer, team, and myself. We weren't all speaking the same language, therefore misunderstood each other's needs. Everyone interpreted what the other said in their own way and this led to a communication breakdown, and ultimately to a bad result.

I used a technique called Acceptance Test-Driven Development (ATDD), which I learned from Ken Pugh's (2010) book called *Lean-Agile Acceptance Test-Driven-Development (Net Objectives Lean-Agile Series)* to change the way we communicated. I used it from the moment we needed it to the final delivery. The result was immediate: there was no longer any dissatisfaction on the part of the customer. There was also no more finger-pointing or time spent on trying to figure out who was to blame. When a problem or error occurred, we simply solved the situation together.

The entire team adopted the technique, which inspired other teams to do the same. I even gave a speech about it at a public event. The key to this positive change lies in how I face problems and obstacles, using a creative rather than reactive attitude.

REACTIVE AND CREATIVE POSITIONS IN ACTION

In Chapter 2, *What are the conditions to be a hero?* the conditions that define a hero are outlined, with the ten behaviors to watch out for. I also highlighted the difference between being a hero and not being a hero, which is determined by whether these behaviors can be observed from day-to-day.

With the new creative positions (Challenger, Coach, and Creator), these behaviors are much less present. But we still need to remain vigilant since old reactive behaviors (Persecutor, Rescuer, and Victim) can return if we forget about them. When a reactive behavior becomes more and more present in everyday life, we need to focus on its equivalent creative behavior.

The following table compares those reactive and creative behaviors:

Table 9.4-Reactive versus creative behaviors

Reactive Behavior	Creative Behavior
Working alone	Teamwork (or at least in a pair)
Keep information to yourself	Share information with colleagues
Do not take vacation	Take time to rest
Work outside of work hours	Work during normal office hours
Making yourself indispensable	Diversify the team members' skills
Be the only person who can solve a problem	Involve the team in the resolution of a problem
Endure their misfortunes	Talk about their problems and count of continuous improvement
Think that no one could understand what they do	Take the necessary time to explain to their coworkers
Get the most individual credit possible	Have success as part of a team

Although creative behaviors are more desirable, reactive behaviors are not completely inappropriate. What matters is to recognize them and not hold onto them.

Reactive (Persecutor, Rescuer, Victim) and creative (Challenger, Coach, Creator) positions are therefore always present, no matter the circumstances. Employees move from one to another depending on the situations, problems, or projects.

One reason for this constant movement between creative and reactive positions is the presence of the VUCA ("Volatility, Uncertainty, Complexity, and Ambiguity", n.d.), which forces companies and employees to adapt. According to Warren Bennis and Burt Nanus's leadership theory, there are four elements to consider:

- **Volatility**: Anything that changes quickly, is short-lived (temporary).
- **Uncertainty**: The unknown and the unpredictable.

- **Complexity**: Technologies, humans and situations are ever more complex.
- **Ambiguity**: Confusion, misunderstanding, and vagueness.

Over the years, technology has become more complex. Customers want more customization, changes occur faster than our ability to integrate them, the complexity of work a company does means we can't control the unpredictable. What is true today may not be true tomorrow. The Covid-19 pandemic is a prime example of a VUCA that threatened multiple companies.

The response to VUCA differs from one company to another, but the most common response is to call upon their heroes.

However, being reactive to VUCA is not necessarily a bad reaction since it's impossible to predict the future. For example, acting spontaneously to solve a problem situation helps to avoid complications for the company. Once the situation is stabilized, one can adopt a creative position to learn from it and avoid repeating the problem. Reactive and creative positions then become useful within the company.

Nevertheless, VUCA cannot be avoided completely: it must be welcomed. A company that tries to avoid all VUCA-related situations only develops its responsiveness, and therefore relies on a culture of heroes to resist. With creative positions in place, the company develops its adaptability, allowing it to become innovative and use continuous improvement to adjust to the company's new reality.

The adaptability of a company is a necessary mixture of responsiveness and creativity.

Being only reactive or only creative is not the way to manage VUCA. You need to look for the advantages of both reactivity and creativity. There will inevitably be disadvantages to both. The important thing is to recognize them and know when to use the right approach.

Table 9.5—Adaptability contains reactivity and creativity

Adaptability		
	Reactivity	Creativity
Advantages	Fast	Receptive to change
	Short term	Collaboration
	Decisive	Long term
Disadvantages	Overspecialization	Slow
	Resistance to change	Risky
	Individualism	Unstable

Let's look at an example to help explain the relationship between reactivity and creativity, and how shifting between the two is necessary for greater adaptability within the company.

Let's imagine that the hero suddenly left the company. The team is now unprepared for a priority project due in a few days. Of course, the hero had the knowledge required to complete the project and the team doesn't know what to do about it.

1. We start with the advantages of reactivity. With the tight deadline, the company needs a quick solution. The immediate response would be to ask another hero for help and avoid breaking the commitment with the customer.
2. Once the situation is under control, the company must decide what to do with the team. If they choose to replace the hero, the team remains in reactive mode, avoiding changes and relying on the expertise of one person. Reactive positions

(Persecutor, Rescuer, Victim) will develop even more, and start laboring under the disadvantages of reactivity.

3. The company would do well to adopt creative positions (Challenger, Coach, and Creator) to gain the benefits of creativity. It's an opportunity to accept change in the team's dynamic and find a better solution together such as diversifying the team's skills. It's a long-term solution which helps the team avoid a repeat of the same delicate situation.

4. This solution can take a long time to implement. The team will become unstable when its members are building their skills, which means there will be complex situations that it won't be able to manage (VUCA). There is nothing stopping another team member from leaving the company before the team recovers, which brings us back to square one.

The shift between reactivity and creativity doesn't occur unless the company accepts the disadvantages that will inevitably offset the advantages.

No employee can be creative without taking the time to experiment with new ideas. Innovation is a risky and rarely a quick process. Like how a hero can't just snap his fingers and solve a problem, it requires an expertise and knowledge of the subject. This balance is achieved when the company understands the advantages and disadvantages of reactivity and creativity, and when employees learn to choose the right course of action to use for a given problem.

Reactivity and creativity are useful tools for companies in their day-to-day work. However, the culture of heroes develops when creative positions (Challenger, Coach, and Creator) are barely present, or absent, in the work environment. Developing creative positions is the key to create the movement between reactivity and creativity, enabling greater adaptability within the company.

SUMMARY

The hero must change his perspective on problems or obstacles to develop a new attitude. Rather than seeing them as situations brought to his shoulders, the hero needs to see them as learning opportunities where he can participate to create change.

There are three creative positions to replace those of Persecutor, Rescuer, and Victim.

1. **Challenger**: Creates change and acts as a positive leader.
2. **Coach**: Helps coworkers grow and inspires confidence.
3. **Creator**: Represents innovation and proposes solutions.

The hero shifts from a reactive to a creative mode.

However, VUCA (volatility, uncertainty, complexity, ambiguity) pressures companies, forcing them to adapt. Reactivity and creativity are necessary for companies to develop their adaptability by focusing on the advantages of both modes without being discouraged by the disadvantages.

Shattering the hero culture in the workplace requires courage and boldness. The final chapter looks at an approach to transform corporate culture by integrating the concepts learned from prior chapters.

CHAPTER 10
HOW TO SHATTER THE HERO CULTURE

" One of the most difficult things is not to change society, but to change yourself.

Nelson Mandela

Whether you're the hero or not, you can't wait for others around you to change. The first step in shattering the hero culture is to change your own attitude. The strategies explained in this book will help you make the change so that it impacts the entire company.

However, shattering the hero culture within a company is a gradual process. As an Organizational Facilitator, I guide companies through three separate phases. I facilitate the process and advise workers in their culture training. This is not about implementing a new culture, this is in fact the responsibility of all members within the company.

Figure 10.1—Three phrases of transformation to shatter the hero culture

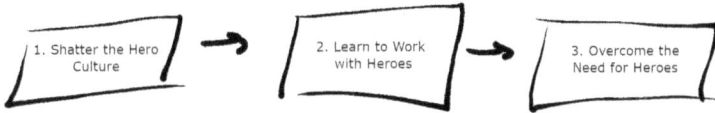

This work is based on Prime/OS™, published as an Open Source, Free Cultural Work via the CC-BY-SA license from Creative Commons. Download the Prime/OS™ Definition Here: http://openspaceagility.com/prime/download-prime/

1. SHATTER THE HERO CULTURE

The first phase is about raising awareness about heroes. We demystify the phenomenon, shed light on the negative effects it has on the company, and we take the first steps to initiate a change in culture.

Using the positions of Persecutor, Rescuer, and Victim, we develop a common language to identify the heroic attitude and its associated effects, such as difficult scheduling, over-specializations, and error avoidance. Chapters 2 and 3 lay the foundation for creating this common language.

When coaching clients, I give a lecture that summarizes the heroic positions and explain the scope of hero culture. This allows participants to gain a common understanding of the subject. The conversation that follows is the first step in shattering the hero culture. Participants can connect the concepts explained with real-life situations in their workplace.

The shatter phase is a time when the company needs to decide whether to go further in changing its culture. The company needs to understand the gaps in its processes, understand what difficulties the employees must face when working with heroes, and understand the benefits of cultural change. At this stage, I work with the company's leaders to understand their "why", which serves as a powerful reminder for the next steps.

Once the why has been identified, it's time to launch the two Open Space meetings. Culture change is achieved by understanding everyone's concerns and making participation voluntary. By creating a unifying and interesting theme, employees are encouraged to participate without feeling obligated. The Open Space meeting is for everyone in the company, from employees to leaders.

All change starts with you. Voluntary participation is the key to support this idea.

I'm often asked to limit the number of participants to save time, but this is not the right way to do it. By limiting the participants, we limit the impact of change on the culture by focusing on a single, more privileged group. Without the other employees there to experience the change, the company will have to repeat the exercise for them, or else it won't be sustainable.

As a guide, this is what I do: I organize and facilitate Open Space meetings. This means I prepare and conduct the events, I reinforce learning after the second Open Space meeting, and I make myself available in between events to support employees in their learning. This approach is *not* broken down into parts because every stage is an integral part of the whole.

Between the two Open Space meetings, there is a period of learning and improvement based on the discussions and action from the first Open Space meeting. The strategies in Chapters 5, 6, and 7 are great examples of actions that can be discussed and used during this period.

It's an opportunity for participants to put into practice what they have decided collaboratively to transform their culture.

Phase 1 takes place over a period of six months but can be extended further if needed. The two Open Space meetings are about three months apart.

Figure 10.2—Phase 1—Shatter the hero culture

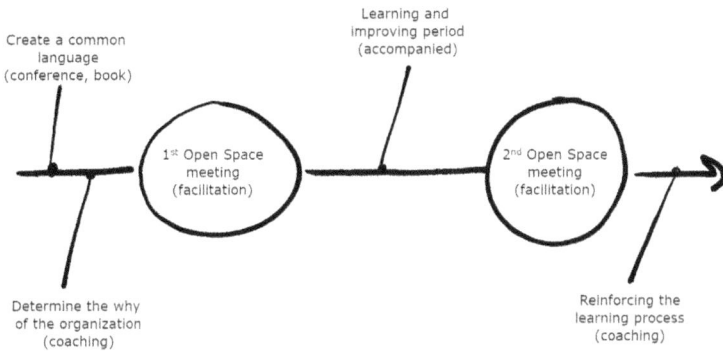

2. LEARN TO WORK WITH HEROES

Phase 2 can begin when the company is ready to transform its culture further by going deep into changing its processes. Unlike Phase 1, the hero phenomenon is well known, and a number of process improvements have already been made, along with some experimentation using the strategies described in Chapters 5, 6, and 7.

To learn to work with heroes, we must consciously develop the new Challenger, Coach, and Creator positions explained in Chapter 9. This phase builds on improving the company's internal processes and procedures mentioned in phase 1.

The stages in Phase 2 are similar to Phase 1: It has two Open Space meetings with a learning period in between. However, the themes addressed are more advanced. The aim is to bend and break certain company rules that don't support the desired internal culture. The learning period is mainly a series of continuous improvements, innovation, and creativity where participants are invited to rewrite the internal culture rules.

The participants are encouraged to challenge the status quo and experiment with their ideas resulting from the Open Space meeting. My coaching focuses on developing opportunities for change with brainstorming and improvement workshops. There is also some mentoring to teach employees the new Challenger, Coach, and Creator positions and help them put their learning into practice.

The second Open Space meeting consolidates and shares the new internal culture among all participants. They discuss what worked and didn't work, and decide on new ideas to try over the next few months.

Every six months, an Open Space meeting is organized. Phase 2 is usually completed within one year. Compared with Phase 1, a longer period of experimentation and learning is required in between Open Space meetings. Finding better ways of doing things requires several cycles of continuous improvements. The first idea may not be adopted, so you need to try or experiment multiple times to find the right one.

Figure 10.3—Phase 2: Learn to work with heroes

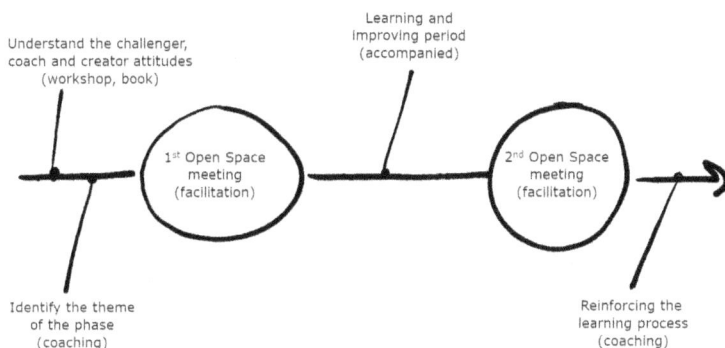

3. OVERCOME THE NEED FOR HEROES

By Phase 3, the company has succeeded to shatter the hero culture and has established a new corporate culture. The company knows that they must keep organizing activities to maintain the status quo and improve its culture. Without regular maintenance, the hero culture is likely to return.

As mentioned in Chapter 9, the company has become adaptable through creative positions (Challenger, Coach, Creator). It has matured enough to recognize the need for an Open Space meeting whenever it is necessary.

Open Space meetings are organized whenever a cultural theme is identified since the approach has now become familiar. The themes are more specific and adapted to the events that occur in the company. The VUCA (volatility, uncertainty, complexity, ambiguity) of the market, mentioned in Chapter 9, is a good source for guidance to initiate an Open Space meeting.

I only support the organization and facilitation of the Open Space meeting in this phase. The company is autonomous in its development, so the support offered in

Phase 3 is mainly giving advice on what could be tackled next.

Figure 10.4—Phase 3: Overcome the Need for Heroes

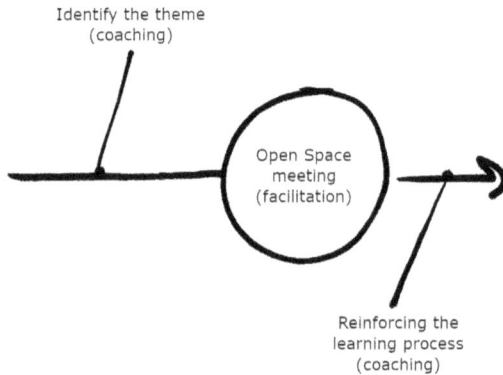

Identify the theme
(coaching)

Open Space
meeting
(facilitation)

Reinforcing the
learning process
(coaching)

Each phase has a clear objective which must be followed. You should *never* rush the transformation. The learning period between Open Space meetings is crucial for employees to learn how to integrate the changes and give the company time to find its balance. If the phases are done too fast, the culture won't change and the "why" identified at the beginning of Phase 1 won't materialize.

Completing the three phases is not a race, but like passing a rank in martial art: you must learn to master a rank before obtaining it, and it takes time. It's a discipline.

MAKING CONNECTIONS BY TELLING YOUR STORY

> I agree with the idea of heroes, but it won't ever change here.

My first client who learned about hero culture

I remember the moment I introduced the hero culture for the first time. My client didn't want to commit to changing the culture. The subject was disturbing, and she didn't understand how to tackle it within the company.

I first had to spark her interest about me, not seek her approval from the get-go.

Start by talking about it around the water cooler. This will help you find allies. Coworkers who have experienced similar situations or noticed problems related to the heroes in the company will be the first to step up to the plate and participate in culture change.

Telling the story of what's currently happening in the company sparks the interest of other coworkers who wish to learn more.

Telling this story doesn't mean complaining or thinking that the 3-phase of culture change will solve every problem. As Dave Gray (2016) says in his book, *Liminal Thinking: Create the Change You Want by Changing the Way You Think*, it's about giving facts, telling relevant anecdotes, and connecting with your coworkers.

Storytelling also means listening to your coworkers' stories.

This story is a source for culture change and a stand against the status quo. By taking a stand with your coworkers, you avoid relying on a hero to change the culture.

Shattering the hero culture requires a personal investment since a company's culture is the sum of all its employees.

The first step is simply to tell your story.

CONCLUSION

> I was really boasting a heroic attitude.

A Former Hero

I'm always excited when I meet clients who tell me about their journey out of hero mode. I can clearly see a difference between their attitude when meeting them and when they say they have moved away from the heroic attitude.

I remember an employee asking me about her manager I had coached. She said, "What did you do to her? She smiled at me today." I could only smile back. This manager had changed her approach with her employees, and showed an openness that invited collaboration. The employees were delighted and surprised by the sudden change within their company.

Another hero I accompanied, an expert in his field, was trapped in his job, kept criticizing the ways of doing things without providing any concrete solution. Basically, this hero wanted to change careers and develop different skills from his expertise, but his professional situation was not adequate for him to make such a change. He was left on his own to work it out. With mentoring, we worked on his attitude, developed new skills, and found another company for him to work. He shifted from a Victim to a creative employee who has now become a coach. This change has allowed him to flourish and serve both himself and his new clients.

The heroic attitude changes when heroes are allowed to grow instead of being seen as a problem that needs to be solved.

One last invitation is for you to tell me your story. No matter if it's a discovery, a challenge, or a success. Sharing will help contribute to the common goal of understanding hero culture in the workplace. My goal is to create a movement, a global community around the hero culture.

Together, we can shatter this culture and create spaces where collaboration, creativity and innovation are genuine.

Please do so via my website. I'll be happy to read your stories and connect with you. (www.simplementcomplexe. com/en/connecter).

Thank you.

COMING SOON

The subject of hero culture is far from over! There will be a sequel to this book that will explore the transformation of corporate culture and how the heroic attitude can change.

To find out more about the hero phenomenon and the release of my next book on the subject, subscribe to my newsletter:

www.simplementcomplexe.com/en/connecter

ACKNOWLEDGMENTS

Writing this book has been quite an adventure! It took me several years to complete. I went through several incomplete drafts and many discussions to validate concepts and clear doubts.

A big thank you to Gilles Duchesne, who was there for the origin of the hero concept. Our valuable conversations help improved my understanding of the heroes. Otherwise, the hero would have only been a problem and not a possibility for change.

The Agile Community remains an international source of incredible people who allowed me to test my conference style. Additionally, I realized how important the subject of heroes is to many more people than I thought! Thank you for reading this book.

During my life, I met several individuals who influenced me and helped me develop the concept of heroes. Thanks to Daniel Mezick for opening my eyes to the world of Open Spaces and the power they hold.

Also, thanks to Gil Broza for the guidance on my path for Agile coaching and helping me believe in myself as a coach. Lastly, I thank the entire team at Ten Directions who helped me develop my qualities as a facilitator and human being.

Writing is a chaotic process. Many people encouraged me through this journey. A special thanks goes to my partner for supporting me through the long writing hours. I'm also grateful for my friends and coworkers who listened to me talk about heroes over and over again.

Thanks go to my editor, Dave Dufour, who helped me glue all the little pieces together and make it across the finish line. Lastly, Félix-Antoine Bourbonnais, Frédéric Rousseau and Francois Tremblay who were the first to read the book and give me valuable feedback.

Once again, thank you.

Dave

BIBLIOGRAPHY

Adams, W. A. & Anderson, R. J. (2016). *Mastering Leadership: An Integrated Framework for Breakthrough Performance and Extraordinary Business Results* (First edition). Wiley.

Adkins, L. (2010). *Coaching Agile Teams: A Companion for ScrumMasters, Agile Coaches, and Project Managers in Transition* (First edition). Addison-Wesley Professional.

Agile Alliance (s.d.). *Mob Programming.* https://www.agilealliance.org/glossary/mob-programming

Beck, K. & Andres, C. (2004). *Extreme Programming Explained: Embrace Change* (Second edition). Addison-Wesley Professional.

Beedle, M., van Bennekum, A., Cockburn, A., Cunningham, W., Fowler, M., Highsmith, J., Hunt, A., Jeffries, R., Kern, J., Marick, B., Martin, R. C., Schwaber, K., Sutherland, J. & Thomas, D. *Manifesto for Agile Software Development.* (2001). https://agilemanifesto.org/

Burgess, M. (2015). *Thinking in Promises: Designing Systems for Cooperation* (First edition). O'Reilly Media.

Brown, B. (2010). *The Power of Vulnerability* [Video]. TED Talks. https://www.ted.com/talks/brene_brown_the_power_of_vulnerability

Broza, G. (2015) *The Agile Mind-Set: Making Agile Processes Work.* Retrieved from https://3pvantage.com/the-agile-mindset-book/

Cirillo, F. (n. d.). *The Pomodoro Technique.* Franceso Cirillo – Work Smarter, Not Harder. https://francescocirillo.com/products/the-pomodoro-technique

Conway, M. E. *How do Committees Invent?* (1968). Mel Conway's Home Page. http://www.melconway.com/Home/Committees_Paper.html

Crispagileacademy. (n. d.). *The Resource Utilization Trap* [Video]. YouTube

Cultural Anthropology. (May 7, 2023). On *Wikipedia.* https://en.wikipedia.org/wiki/Cultural_anthropology

Derby, E. & Larsen, D. (2006). *Agile Retrospectives: Making Good Teams Great* (First edition). Pragmatic Bookshelf.

Dweck, C. S. (2006). *Mindset: The New Psychology of Success.* Ballantine Books.

Emerald, D. (2013). *The Power of TED* (*The Empowerment Dynamic)* (Third edition) Polaris Publishing.

Gil, P., Medjad, N. et Lacroix, P. (2016). *Neuro Learning : les neurosciences au service de la formation.* Eyrolles.

Google. (n.d.) *re: Work Guide: Understand Team Effectiveness.* https://rework.

withgoogle.com/guides/understanding-team-effectiveness/steps/iden
tify-dynamics-of-effective-teams/

Gray, D. (2016). *Liminal Thinking: Create the Change You Want by Changing the Way You Think* (First edition). Two Waves Books.

Karoshi. (May 10, 2023). On *Wikipedia*. https://en.wikipedia.org/wiki/Karoshi

Karpman, S. B. (s. d.). [Introduction where the Karpman triangle is]. *Karpman Drama Triangle*. com. https://www.karpmandramatriangle.com/

Karpman, S. (2014). *A Game Free Life: The definitive book on the Drama Triangle and Compassion Triangle by the originator and author*. Drama Triangle Publications.

Kniberg, H. (2011) *Multitasking Name Game*. Crisp. https://www.crisp.se/gratis-material-och-guider/multitasking-name-game

Laloux, F. (2014). *Reinventing Organizations: A Guide to Creating Organizations Inspired by the Next Stage in Human Consciousness* (First edition). Nelson Parker.

Loi de Conway. (January 19, 2023). On *Wikipedia*. https://fr.wikipedia.org/wiki/Loi_de_Conway

Management 3.0. (n. d.) *Team Competency Matrix*. https://management30.com/practice/competency-matrix/

McNamara, R. (2013) *The Elegant Self: A Radical Approach to Personal Evolution for Greater Influence In Life*. Performance Integral.

Mezick, D. (2012). *The Culture Game: Tools for the Agile Manager*. FreeStanding Press.

Mezick, D. (2014). *Prime O/S*. OpenSpace Agility. https://openspaceagility.com/prime/download-prime/

Patton, J. *User Story Mapping*. (s. d.). Jeff Patton & Associates. https://www.jpattonassociates.com/story-mapping/

PDCA. (April 17, 2023). On *Wikipedia*. https://en.wikipedia.org/wiki/PDCA

Pugh, K. (2010). *Lean-Agile Acceptance Test-Driven-Development: Better Software Through Collaboration (Net Objectives Lean-Agile Series)* (First edition). Addison-Wesley Professional.

Rothman, J. (2016). *Manage Your Project Portfolio: Increase Your Capacity and Finish More Projects* (Second edition). Pragmatic Bookshelf.

Sheridan, R. (2013). *Joy, Inc.: How We Built a Workplace People Love*. Portfolio.

Slaughter, R. (Ed.) (2010). *Failure: The secret to success*.

Syndrome de l'imposteur. (March 26, 2023). On *Wikipedia*. https://fr.wikipedia.org/wiki/Syndrome_de_l%27imposteur

The 4 Ways of Leading. (n. d.). Conscious Leadership Group. Retrieved from https://conscious.is/excercises-guides/the-4-ways-of-leading

Volatility, Uncertainty, Complexity and Ambiguity. (April 23, 2023). On *Wiki-*

pedia.   https://en.wikipedia.org/wiki/Volatility,_uncertainty,_complexi
ty_and_ambiguity

RESOURCES

All the resources including references, exercises, templates, and links are available online:

https://www.simplementcomplexe.com/en/heros-ressources

BIOGRAPHY

Certified Integral Facilitator®, Dave Jacques is an Agile coach and facilitator who strives to simplify the complex. He sets himself apart with his human approach, leading to lasting change and a high level of collaboration in the companies he helps.

Since 2014, he's helped government organizations, insurance companies, SMEs, non-profits, and start-ups to create a better work environment. Dave facilitates the development culture with open communication, trust, and a commitment to achieving goals. As a guest speaker at Agile academic and corporate events, he speaks authentically and colorfully to ensure everyone understands.

Shatter the Hero Culture is the first book to create a movement towards a corporate culture where collaboration, creativity, and innovation are real and achievable.

Dave is a tea lover who is always ready to talk while sipping on a cup of hot tea. Contact him via www.simple mentcomplexe.com